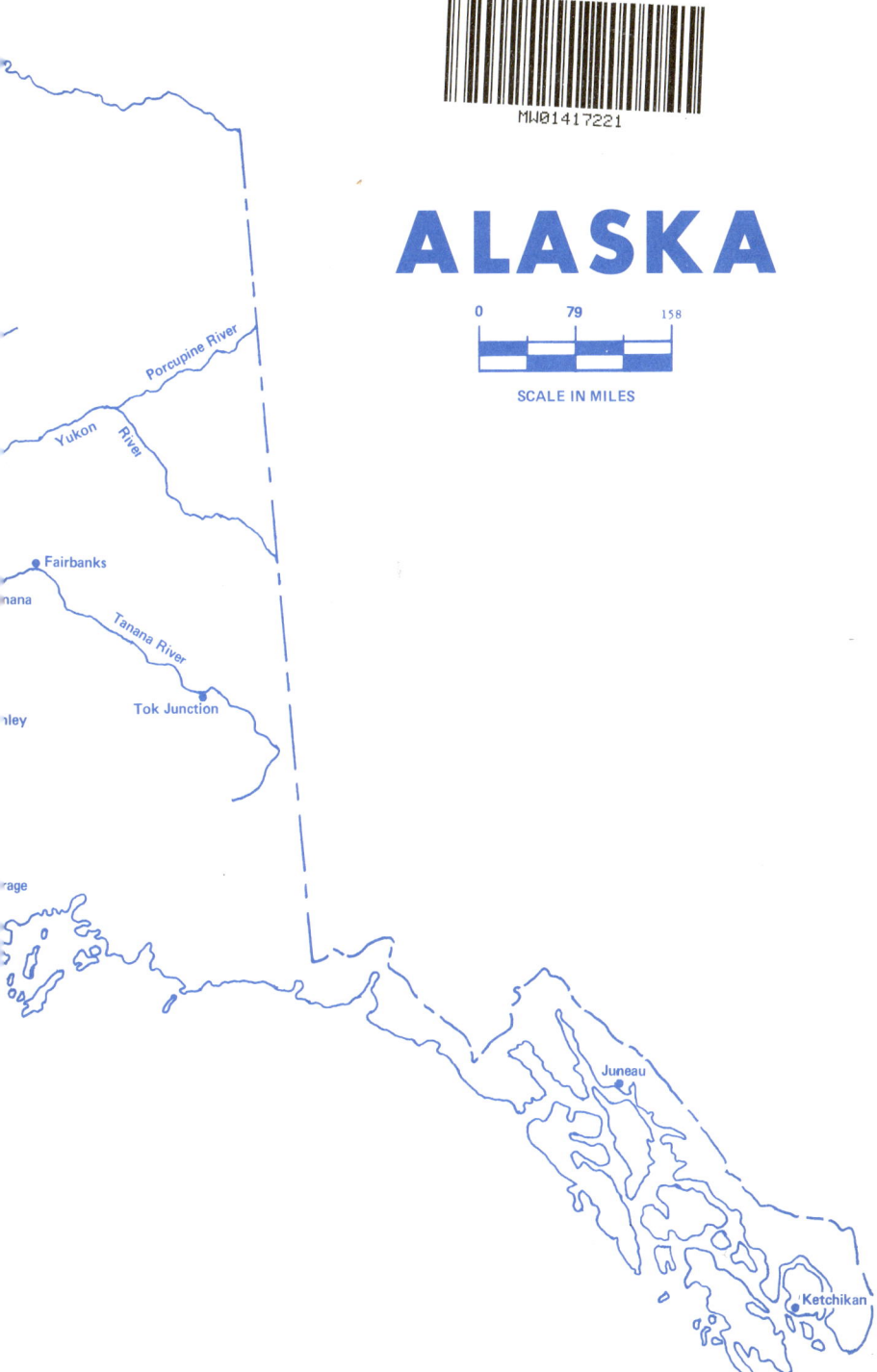

TRAINING AND RACING SLED DOGS

George Attla and his leader Tex after winning his first World Championship race, Anchorage, Alaska, 1958. (Photograph courtesy of Forrest and Helen Shields.)

EVERYTHING I KNOW ABOUT TRAINING AND RACING SLED DOGS

by
GEORGE ATTLA
1972 World Champion

with
Bella Levorsen

Copyright ©1974 by Arner Publications

All rights reserved. No part of this book may be reproduced or transmitted in any form or by any means, electronic or mechanical including photo copying, recording, or by any information storage and retrieval system, without permission in writing from the publisher.

Library of Congress Catalog Card Number: 74-83255

ISBN: 0-914124-02-1

Second Edition 1974

Design by Dorothy Shackley

Arner Publications, Rome, NY

Printed in the United States of America

ARNER
PUBLICATIONS, INC.

ACKNOWLEDGEMENT

I wish to acknowledge the help given to the compiling of this book by Harris Dunlap, Mel Fishback, Kent Allender, and Pat Daniels. Nancy Link and Marge McLucas helped take off tapes. Critical reading of the manuscript was done by The Reverend Donald Hart, John Levorsen, Joan McGee—all of Alaska—and Mel Fishback, Chris Drake, and Mr. and Mrs. Claude Phelan of California.

Daphne Levorsen typed the final manuscript and did the drawings.

Maxine Vehlow took her photographs especially for use here.

Mr. William H. Freeman of Freeman, Cooper and Company, Publishers, San Francisco gave valuable advice about and help with publication.

Special mention for unfailing support must go to my husband, Bob; my daughter Daphne; my mother, Emily Fogelman, and George's wife, Karen Attla.

So many other people also helped in such diverse ways that it would take a whole page just to list them all.

To each and every one of you, my sincere thanks.

Bella Levorsen

CONTENTS

PREFACE	11
HUSLIA	22
GREAT DOGS AND RACES OF YESTERDAY	30
TRAINING PHILOSOPHY	44
FALL TRAINING SCHEDULE	47
WINTER TRAINING	60
QUESTIONS AND ANSWERS	65
Breeding	66
Puppies	72
Build	77
Feeding and Watering	81
Changing Owners	86
Equipment—Sleds, Lines, Harnesses, Accessories	90

Dog Psychology	102
Attitude in Harness	107
Team Make-up	110
Leaders and Leader Training	113
Passing	126
Stopping	129
Loafers	130
Bad Habits	132
Riding the Sled	135
Trails	139
Lame Dogs	141
Health	144
Travel	147
Race Strategy	148
THE BIG PLAN	166
APPENDIX	171
1972 Racing Record	173
Glossary	175
Racing Sled Diagram	180
Dog Team Nomenclature	181

ILLUSTRATIONS

George Attla and his leader Tex.	2
Huslia, as seen from the front of George's house.	13
George, Bill and friends take a breather.	15
Inspecting a trap.	16
Bill, George and beaver.	16
Enjoying a dried fish.	17
Dog stew cooking.	17
Trapping cabin.	18
On guard.	19
"Warm your hands around your mug of coffee."	21
George Junior, Bill Sturdevant, George Senior, and Eliza Attla.	27
George with Mr. and Mrs. Grier of Penney's.	37
Rendezvous, 1969.	37
1970 North American in Fairbanks.	38
1971 North American.	39
After the 1972 North American Championship. (2)	40
The competition. (2)	41
"But if I holler 'Get Up!' " (2)	56

Letter from George.	57
George being congratulated.	65
George and friends behind his house.	72
Tuffy's son, Ganja.	78
Jarvi.	79
Little Toughie.	79
"...right around five o'clock every night."	82
Racing Breakfast.	85
Sled and dog truck.	92
Harness and lines, 1970 Rendezvous.	94
George's towline.	97
George's snow hook.	99
"I always carry oranges."	101
Rendezvous 1972, Grover and Jarvi in lead.	106
Edwin Simon and Sammy Sam.	114
Bessie and Chief Henry.	114
"...sometimes you get in the middle of a big lake."	118
Nellie and Bill William's Judy, 1962.	120
Tuffy in retirement.	120
Fourth Avenue.	137
"...swing your foot."	137
Drawing for position.	150
At the starting line, 1970 Rendezvous. (3)	152-153
"How I run the 20 mile race."	161
"If I'm pacing myself..." (3)	162-163
Letter from George.	165
Crossing the finish line, 1972 Rendezvous.	172
George and Grover.	172
Racing sled.	180
Dog team.	181

PREFACE
by Bella Levorsen

I met George Attla in February, 1966. This was our family's first winter in Alaska. We called Trinidad in the West Indies "home," so knew little about sled dogs and less about keeping warm in an Arctic winter. Nevertheless, we were trying to get a sled dog team together. Our tutor was Bill Sturdevant, a 20 year old musher from Anchorage. The night after the big Fur Rendezvous race, we and several out-of-town mushers like Bergman Sam were having coffee at Bill's house. Bergman was returning home to Huslia with his dogs the next morning. Huslia is a small Indian village in the middle of Alaska about 50 miles from the Arctic Circle.

At 10 P.M. my husband, Bob, got the idea that Bill should go to Huslia with Bergman to try to pick up some dogs to race in the coming North American Championship race in Fairbanks. Bob asked if I wanted to go along. At 6 A.M. the three of us plus 12 dogs, two sleds and several 50 pound sacks of dog food, were on our way.

My first hint of conditions in the Alaskan wilderness

came at Galena where we changed from the big Anchorage plane to a Wien one-engined bush-hopper. I got to sit with the pilot. After I got in, the sacks of dog food were put aboard. The airline crates had to be left in Galena so the dogs were put aboard, loose, on top of the food. The sleds went on top of the dogs, who squirmed around to avoid runners and brakes. Finally Bergman and Bill wiggled in among the dogs and the sleds.

At Huslia the whole town turned out to meet the plane. Each man seemed to claim and take off with a dog that belonged to him. Bergman took off with a case of whiskey that he had smuggled in for his friends. (They drank the whole case that evening.) Bill just took off. I was left standing by the plane. A group of women there were hesitant, but smiling. One of them motioned to a snowmobile which I was obviously supposed to get on. I was taken to what was the village store, post office and private residence. Someone took my bag to a room and said, in English, that this was where I was to stay. From what I had seen of Huslia already, I had certainly not expected a private room. A small sign stated that this building was also the hotel, although at the end of my visit when I offered to pay, my hosts would accept nothing.

After a most welcome cup of tea, the gathered assemblage of women who were waiting for the mail to be distributed cautiously inquired who I was and what I was doing in Huslia. They knew Bill was looking for dogs, but why would he bring along his mother? When I said I was the sponsor, then the picture became clear. They knew what a sponsor was all right. When I added that we were supposed to be looking for George Attla because Bill was a friend of his, everyone nodded and smiled and became downright friendly. I didn't know it at the time, but George was Chief of the village. I was told that George was out with a group of men on a caribou hunt.

Since there seemed to be nothing else to do right then, I walked around the village wondering where Bill was and gathering quite a crowd of tittering children behind me.

Huslia, as seen from in front of George's house.

Eventually Bill popped out of a doorway and beckoned to me to come in the house. Inside were a group of rugged-looking men who fell silent as I entered. Not a woman or child was in sight. One of the men was sitting on a gory and frozen caribou. He got up and pushed it out of sight behind the stove as Bill introduced us. Here, towering above me, was Alaska's folk hero, George Attla. I had heard tales of his background, his racing expertise and his dog-dealings ever since I had reached Alaska. I was awed and speechless. I finally mumbled something and then backed as inconspicuously as possible into a corner. The men started talking in their Athabascan dialect again.

Bill informed me they were talking about dogs. Only one race team was available, and it was being trained by Lucien Sam in the hope that he could get together enough money to enter the Fairbanks race in four weeks. Bill asked me if I would agree to sending this team into Fairbanks where Lucien would race it, and then Bill would get it the following week to race in Tok. I agreed. Business taken care of, Lucien and the men left with big smiles on their faces.

Bill and George started chatting like the old friends that they were, and I unshrunk out of the corner.

Turned out that George was also going into Fairbanks, not with dogs, but on village business. The next plane to anywhere was not for four days, so he was going to run his trapline first. He could get a team together for Bill and they would both go. Bill turned and asked if I wanted to go with them. At that remark, George just about turned green under his tan and gave me a look that withered me right back into the corner again. Even Bill didn't know that the Indians seldom took their own women on a trip like that, let alone a white woman. But I had seen Huslia, several times over, and George seemed less of a menace right then than the prospect of sitting alone in the village for four days. So I said I would go. At Bill's assuring him that I was a very hardy type — Bill didn't really know if I was or I wasn't — George quickly recovered his composure, and like the gentleman he is, invited us both to supper.

At the word "supper," George's wife, Shirley, and several children appeared. They stood watching, but didn't eat with us. The meal was stewed beaver which George and Bill ate with their fingers. Shirley found a fork for me. The beaver was delicious, like a cross between beef and lamb. After supper the three of us walked over to the community room where a whole townful of boisterously happy Indians had gathered.

Next morning when my host and hostess found out about the trapline trip, they just shook their heads, muttered "cold" and dug around to get me some warmer clothes. The temperature outside was 45 below zero.

Both teams of 14 dogs each were harnessed and the sleds were loaded when I got to George's house. George was carrying most of the gear; Bill had a sack of dried fish, the dog chains and me. Dried fish make a pretty good pillow. The chains were cold. George went first and we followed. About ten miles out, one of our dogs got so tired he dropped and couldn't get up. We had to stop to unhitch him. I got this job, but then I was reluctant to leave this

George, Bill and teams take a breather.

poor dog lying out there by himself on the frozen wastes. I was sure he would die. I was arguing about this with Bill as the sled inched further and further down the trail. I suddenly realized that Bill couldn't hold the team any longer as it was eager to chase George. It came over me that it wasn't going to be just the dog out there alone, but me, too. That was the end of the argument, and I ran to catch up to the sled as fast as I could. A few miles later Bill tapped me on the shoulder, smiled and pointed behind him. To my joy there was the friend I had deserted trotting happily along with us, almost between the runners.

About 10 o'clock we came to one of the Attla family's trapping cabins. George was waiting for us. He tied up the loose dog along with another that was tiring too rapidly. He left them each several dried fish.

At noon we came to another cabin where the dogs got a fish for lunch and a rest. George brewed us some tea. We were cold, but in the best of spirits. As the afternoon wore on, the miles got longer and the sun got lower, and I got colder.

Just as the sun was going down, about eight hours and 50 miles after we started, we came upon the final cabin. As quickly as possible George and Bill put out the stake chains and snapped the dogs to them. Then came an outdoor fire with an old oil drum on top of it. Into the drum went snow

Inspecting a trap.

Bill, George and beaver.

Enjoying a dried fish.

Dog stew cooking.

and some frozen animals which had been trapped and skinned earlier and stored in the cache. George chopped them up with an ax, entrails and all. An hour later the mixture was a succulent stew for the dogs.

While it had been cooking we had been unloading the sleds, and George had started a fire in the cabin and put a pot of snow on the stove. Note that George had done most everything. Bill had been some help, but I had mostly stumbled around half congealed.

The cabin was a one room affair made of logs, with the cracks stuffed with mud and moss. George's family had built this cabin when he was a boy. The furniture consisted of a kitchen table and a bunk covered with a moose hide. Two Chevron oil cans cut in half and a big block of wood served as chairs. A good supply of fire wood, complete with those little carved-up starter sticks, was next to the stove, and a cabinet was stocked with staples. No lock was on the door. George said they always left their cabins this way in case someone came along in desperate need of food and shelter.

After a good dinner of more stewed beaver, Bill and George continued their chattering of the night before. I took to my sleeping bag on the moose-covered bunk with my bottle of Trinidad rum. Neither of them wanted any rum, but this was one time I didn't mind drinking alone. I fell asleep listening to their laughter.

Trapping cabin where we spent two nights.

On Guard

During the night the room got cold. If possible, I was even colder than the day before. At first light I opened my eyes and peeped out of my sleeping bag to watch George get up and light the fire. I didn't volunteer to help.

The day was glorious. Bill and George took their teams and raced each other from trap to trap like a couple of kids. I stayed and cleaned the cabin, kept a pot of snow melting on the stove and tried out a pair of snowshoes. I was glad no one was watching. George had left a couple of dogs behind which he said were tired. I finally realized that they were not tired but had been left with me to discourage any curious moose or wolves. By evening I had the dog stew fire laid and the oil drum full of snow. I didn't attempt the frozen animal and ax bit. The tea was ready when they got in at dusk. George grudgingly allowed as how I didn't make too bad a squaw for two days' practice.

That evening after dinner the wind was blowing and the dogs were howling. George said at first that they were howling at nearby wolves but then changed his story to that they were howling because a couple of females were in season. I never did know which it really was. I was finally thawed out and relaxed so joined in the kidding. George was drinking tea and skinning a wolverine he had caught. The latter was a little hard to take, but it was either sit there or go outside with the dogs and the wolves. Not much choice.

19

Such was the setting in which this book was first born. I had been a dog obedience trainer for many years so was interested in how George trained his dogs. I asked him question after question which he patiently answered. He was really thinking back and talking to himself when he was telling how after every race he sat alone and analyzed the performance of each dog to see how it could be improved. During his musing he suddenly returned to the present, looked at me and said something I had first heard years before from Blanche Saunders, the queen of American obedience trainers. "You know, Bella, the dog is never wrong."

Three years later I found that a lot of mushers in the Lower 48 were in awe of the fact that we knew George Attla. They kept asking me what George would do about this and what would he do about that. So I wrote George and asked him if he would be interested in putting his knowledge of dog training on tape so that I could write it up in book form. He would.

This information has been gathered over a period of more than two years. All in all George recorded 17 rolls of tape, doing a little whenever he was in the mood, wherever he happened to be — Huslia, Anchorage, Minnesota, on the Yukon. Sometimes when he was out of tape, he wrote letters. The last fill-in scraps of information were gleaned by my talking with him and watching him in action when we were together in the Midwest this winter.

We started with a set of questions compiled from those asked by several mushers. George answers most of them in the question and answer section. Other answers are handled in narrative form. But much of the information in the text he offered spontaneously as the thoughts came to him.

The chapter on Huslia was done by The Reverend Donald Hart of Anchorage, who with his wife, Betty, and three children put in a five year tour of service in Huslia as Episcopal minister to the village. He was there from 1964 to 1969.

He writes, "My friendship with George was based on the simple routines of life. I've cut wood with him, hunted caribou together, kibbitzed with him while he built sleds,

"Warm your hands around your mug of coffee."

helped him out on the village council while he was Chief — a thousand contacts of daily life."

So join us. Warm your hands around your mug of coffee. Let your mind journey to the frozen Arctic. Listen in on George talking dogs, as the snow drifts outside and the huskies howl in the moonlight.

HUSLIA

by The Reverend Donald Hart

In the gravel banks and thawing mud of the Koyukuk and Huslia Rivers can be found the huge tusks of the woolly mammoth. The house of an ancient, giant beaver has also been found. In the forests and swamps of this long-gone age of giantism, the great bear and a moose even larger than his present ancestors moved with a grandeur which pushes our imaginations to their limits. But more significant than the size of these animals, comes the question, "Was man present?" Then, too, was it in this age that the first contacts between man and dog, the beginnings of a vital relationship, took place? Few records remain of early man in this country of tundra and meandering river. When did man first come? Did he find the dog already here, or did they come together? We may never know. But on one point the record is very clear, written in present day Huslia and dozens of other Alaskan villages, that the relationship between man and dog has been a key to survival, and has contributed to a rich and satisfying life-style.

On August 16, 1885, Lt. H.T. Allen, USA, recorded the

Koyukan Indian name "Husliakakat River," meaning "mouth of the Huslia." (*Dictionary of Alaska Place Names,* Donald J. Orth, Geological Survery Professional Paper 567, Washington, 1967. p. 439) It was after this stream which flows into the Koyukuk River a mile away that the citizens of Huslia named their village.

Huslia is 4,200 miles directly north of Honolulu. The nearest village is 60 air miles away. The last road ends just out of Fairbanks, some 260 miles to the east and south. Huslia joins up with the rest of the world by airplane, by an incredibly intricate trail system made for dogs and now snow machine, and by the Koyukuk River, which flows down from the Brooks Range as a major northern tributary of the Yukon River.

With all of its remote statistics — and few other places in the entire world compare with Huslia's remoteness — this community is home in the richest sense of the word for those with roots there. Its geography places Huslia on the border between the territory of the Indians of the Interior and the territory of the Eskimos of the Arctic Coast. Many stories exist of partnerships, trading relationships and visiting which have taken place between the Athabascan Indians of Huslia and the Eskimos of the Kobuk River area. But in spite of these encounters with the Eskimos, Huslia's culture has remained completely Indian.

The high sand bluff, on which Huslia is built, is part of a ridge running almost the entire length of a vast plain bounded by the Brooks Range foothills to the north and the Yukon River to the south. This ridge has been important in the lives of many generations because it was always a refuge in spring floodings. The ground drained well so it was a natural place for burying the dead. Most of the families moved to Huslia in the late forties and early fifties when the old village of Cutoff, four miles away, became uninhabitable because of wet ground. The people moved themselves with no help from government agencies. Life in the new village was immediately marked by a fierce pride and independence and desire for achievement.

Routines of life in the new community changed very little, except for the introduction of a permanent school and church. Trapping was the primary economy. The people lived off the land, depending on the fish, the moose and caribou, and the smaller animals for almost all their food and the basic winter clothing. The land was good to them, and they were good to the land.

The population fluctuates depending on the season, work available in the larger towns, trapping possibilities, the dog racing carnivals. If everyone were ever at home at one time, 168 people could be counted. But in the summer most of the men are away finding employment, and in the winter the teenage children are gone to high schools and a growing number to colleges.

Today Huslia men serve in Viet Nam and South Korea and Germany. They live all over Alaska as well as in Kansas and California. Some have moved to the big cities or other states, been successful at making a good living and then returned to Huslia because they preferred the life-style of their village to that of any other place. Today Huslians live in Huslia because they want to be there, not because they have no place else to go.

The geography of Huslia remains remote. The people do not. As new ideas, new skills, new dreams filter back home, life is changing. There are still those who can seek out the straight-grained birch for sleds and snowshoes. Still men trap and hunt by dog team. Still women tan moose skins and furs to keep their families in snow boots and parkas. Still the older generation tells the long stories of their heritage in their native Athabascan Indian language. But the necessity for doing these things has grown much less. The arts and crafts, so vital to a culture, are not easily handed down to kids who spend 9/12ths of the year in school somewhere else. But some of these young people, like John Sackett, serve their village and their heritage in a way never known to their parents. John was elected to the State Legislature while he was still a student at the University of Alaska.

The many seasons in Huslia each bring their own recurring

events. The salmon run up to Koyukuk the first week in July. The community responds in a tremendous effort to catch fish for the family table and dry enough for a winter's supply of dog food. By the first week of September the leaves are flying, ice begins forming along the edges of the small lakes, and the moose are prime. Snow comes in earnest the first couple of weeks in October, and so does the solid ice. Every house in town heats with a wood stove so this is the time to make sure cords of wood are ready for the deepening cold. November starts the trapping and bear hunting seasons. Caribou file through the mountain passes in December and January, and men and dogs and snow machines may be gone a week and several hundred miles in the darkest and coldest weather.

The lengthening days mean beaver trapping and then boat building. The month of May begins with several feet of snow still on the ground. In two weeks "ground time" is back, kids are shooting marbles in the dust, dogs are tied for the summer, new mosquitoes dance in the warm sunlight, and fish nets are being mended. There is the time in the midst of all this when the thermometer reaches 70 above for the first time and everyone has heat exhaustion. Then it goes to 90. In the winter everyone freezes the first time the temperature goes down to 20 below. Then it sticks at 60 below for a week and 40 below seems warm.

There is the time when the sick must be evacuated to the hospital 100 miles away, and no planes are flying. There is the time when the high school kids return in the spring and joy reigns in every home. The mail plane comes with word that a grandson is wounded nearly 9,000 miles away in South East Asia, and sadness descends upon every home. There is a time for story-telling. A time for games. A time for mushing.

Huslia has its own race at New Year's. The holiday is a carnival of activities. Visitors come from neighboring villages to join in dances and potlatches. No one is left out. Every age can enter the foot races and snowshoe races, the tug-of-war, and the shooting contest. Huslia even has to admit to a short snow machine race! But the crowning events are the dog team races. Each village puts on only one race a year for men and one for women. Roughly 10 teams race between 16 and 24 miles. For children, races are held every weekend, but this one is the big one. The rising crescendo of excitement coming from Huslia's dog yards on New Year's Day must send shudders of terror into every moose for ten miles. But for people and dogs this is a glorious moment. Out of these dog yards have come winning teams in every major race held in Alaska throughout the years. Out of these dog yards have come individual dogs to race on the winning teams in almost every major race throughout the country.

The first big race of the year which attracts mushers from all over Alaska and the Lower 49 is usually the State Championship race at Kenai-Soldotna. The temperature in Kenai in early February can be 80 degrees warmer than in Huslia. Hard on racing dogs! Also, the dogs have been training on trails running across lakes and through stands of jack spruce with only an occasional moose or ptarmigan to break the monotony. In Kenai they run parallel to one of Alaska's major highways which during race time becomes jammed with traffic. A few weeks later the scene shifts to Anchorage and the Fur Rendezvous. Almost half the race is run within the city, crossing and recrossing highways, and at the beginning and end using the city streets for a trail. Thousands of people line the final mile or two. Flashbulbs pop. Cheering, cars, motorcycles, snow machines, loose pet dogs, discarded hot dogs — all are there as men and teams pour out every ounce of strength and courage to make the best time. This is "carnival" in all its best and worst aspects.

By mid-March racing moves to the North American Championship race at Fairbanks. This time the trail is mostly in the countryside, and Huslia dogs must be grateful. The Race of Champions in Tok towards the end of March, smaller races at Nenana, Tanana, Galena and Hughes round out the season by mid-April. When the dogs come home they are greeted with a howling welcome from those left behind. And all of Huslia reruns every race with her mushers.

George Junior, Bill Sturdevant, George Senior, Eliza Attla in front of one of the Attla family's trapping cabins, 1966.

Winners from Huslia — Jimmie Huntington, Cue Bifelt, Warner Vent, Bergman Sam and George Attla, Jr. — all have helped make the community famous for its dogs and mushers and have brought a fierce pride to its citizens. The name of a good dog, the year of a winning team; no one forgets these things. Each musher has his story. None has won his races easily. To this degree nothing is unusual about George Attla. Yet, obviously, to know George, to see him in action, to hear him speak and share his experiences is to meet a unique person.

George was born in August, 1933 to George, Sr. and Eliza Attla when his family was down river at the village of Koyukuk fishing for their winter supply. He is one of five brothers and three sisters. In those days most families lived in several different places depending on the season. A fish camp, three or four trapping and hunting cabins spaced out to have about a day's travel with dog team between them, and the town house in the old village of Cutoff were all home. George grew up in all of them as his family moved from camp to camp and in and out of town. Mobility and prosperity go hand in hand in trapping-hunting societies, so undoubtedly the sound of excited dogs being harnessed filled George's earliest awareness.

Like many others of his generation, George contracted tuberculosis. The dread of this disease can hardly be imagined with today's medicines. Almost every family which eventually settled in Huslia could point to relatives in their past who had died from this killer. But in the early forties when symptoms were identified in George, Public Health was beginning the monumental task of bringing the beast under control. George was eight years old when he first went out to the hospital at Tanana for a six months stay. He went home, and then out to Tanana again for a two year stretch. George had had no formal schooling. His family spoke only their own Athabascan Indian language. Now in this second period in the hospital, he learned to speak, read and write English — and his school days were ended. His third stay, in the Mount Edgecumbe Hospital near Sitka, lasted two and a half years. When his family finally received him back for good, he was in his mid-teens. He had recovered. But not without scars. The kind of tuberculosis George had centered in his right leg bone around his knee. In order to allow him a chance to walk again, a bone fusion was done which permanently locked the knee joint. George did walk again. Not only that, but he quickly developed a way to run with a peculiar swinging action. Soon, on one of the hundreds of trails around Huslia, that famous Attla "kick" began to turn out the miles behind a fast-moving sled.

The last few years George has had to undergo more rounds with doctors and hospitals. This time it is one eye that is bothered by glaucoma.

Dog team racing has come a long way since the first Huslia dogs and men joined in competition. Today's events, on the surface, seem to have little semblance to the time Jimmie Huntington mushed his dogs over half way from the banks of the Koyukuk into Fairbanks for a grueling, two-day, 80 mile endurance race. Now all the aspects of big business are present, with money for buying dogs and vitamins and enriched feed and being able to afford the free time for training making a difference in who wins. But still essential at the finish line, no matter rich or poor, is tremendous individual effort and that mysterious, profound relationship between man and dog.

Who was the man to first reach out his hand in friendly greeting to the first sniff of dog? The beginnings of this incredibly faithful relationship are covered in the drifts of time. But the undeniable fact that this partnership is alive and well howls forth from the dog yards of Huslia.

GREAT DOGS AND RACES OF YESTERDAY

by George Attla

We will get into dog racing now.

Jimmy Huntington was the trailblazer, the first one who came out of Cutoff and started racing. His first race was in 1939, and he placed fourth in Fairbanks. That was an 80 mile race then.

In 1958 when I first raced outside, there was no snowgos then, and there was just unlimited amounts of good dogs. Good dogs all over the village. At that time a 12 dog team was a big team. I didn't really know that much about dogs to begin with, so all I was looking for was just a twelve dog team.

I was the only one that was coming in, so every time one of my dogs would go lame on me, I would go to one of the guys in the village and say, "One of my dogs went lame." It didn't matter who I went to, I knew I would always get the best dog he had. I couldn't remember one dog that I returned that couldn't make the grade. I sort of hate to think back about it, when I think about how hard it is today to come by just that one good dog. So I came down to Anchorage that year with only 12 dogs.

My leader was Tennessee. I was single then and just playing around. If I could get enough fish for my dogs, that was all I was worried about. My brother had a family to support. Everyone in the village was just making a living with his dogs then, just trapping and hauling wood. We didn't keep no more dogs than we needed or that could help us. My brother gave me Tennessee because he was no good for hauling a load. When you were going at a slow pace and there was a big load to haul, his hind end was going to the left and his front end was going to the right. When a dog is pulling this way going at a slow pace, he gets out of balance maybe every 50 feet and slacks off, and he isn't doing nothing until he gets his balance back again. But as far as running goes, Tennessee was really good.

I had him for two years before the Rendezvous, and this dog was just a pet to me. I used to take him everywhere I went. Maybe I went for a walk in the summer and I would take him with me and play with him. He would do anything I would tell him to do. If I told him to swim the creek, he would swim the creek. He was just a companion to me was what he was. I let him get away with a lot of stuff. Actually in the 1958 race, Tennessee was the only dog I owned in the whole team.

The rest of the dogs belonged to my brother Steven Attla, my brother-in-law Georgie Frank, my father and Cue Bifelt. I would say that the most outstanding litter of pups ever produced in Huslia was a litter of seven that belonged to Cue Bifelt. I don't know how many of the seven that Cue ran, but there were four from that litter that Cue loaned out, and they were really outstanding animals. They never got hurt, and they never tired out, and they were eager to go all the time. They had a natural attitude that they just wanted to run. From what I gathered from Sidney Huntington, they were no good as far as trap line dogs go. They didn't make the grade there. Sidney had those dogs one year for trapping and didn't have much use for them. What he didn't like was that when he was checking his traps, these dogs just wouldn't stand still.

I raced them myself in 1958, the first time I raced. The dogs were Red, Tex, Spotty and Scotty. Red and Tex were the leaders. They were really good leaders. Maybe they weren't the best command dogs in the world, but all they wanted to do was run. Every time I hooked them up, they acted as if they were going to tear everything apart. They were just crazy.

It was the third day of the Rendezvous that they led me off the trail downtown. I had only nine dogs left. They saw some stray dog running down a side road, and they took off after it. When I told them to stop and turn around, it didn't mean nothing to them. They were going to get that dog. After they lost sight of the dog, then I got their attention back. Then when I gave them the command to turn around and get me back on the trail where I was supposed to be, they took the command. They weren't bolting. They were just chasing after anything they saw. They were just happy dogs. They took me back on the trail, and we took off again and continued the race.

Spotty was a swing dog. Every time we would hit a road crossing she would let out a yell just from being excited. It seemed like she was just happy to be making the road crossing. I was running 12 dogs that first day, and this would just turn the whole team on. They would really go. There was just no stopping the enthusiasm of that dog. As long as I have driven dogs, she was really unusual.

Scotty was a powerhouse. He was a big dog. As long as I could remember he was a wheel dog. When I drove him, he was always giving everything he had. He was just really eager to run.

I don't really remember how many years those four dogs ran, but almost every time they ran in a team, they won the race. They were only four dogs, but they were the main part of the whole team. There was no way you could break their spirit. When I was running them in '58, if I ran them day after day and mile after mile, every time I would stop they would stand there and lunge and just be crazy to go. I have never seen any of those four dogs tired. Those are the only dogs I have ever seen that way.

I remember the second day of that Rendezvous, I was running my own leader, Tennessee. I was having trouble with him because he was getting pooped out. Actually, what happened was that this dog was just too smart. He had been around a long time before I got him. He had a mind of his own. There was nothing actually wrong with him. He just figured, "Well, this is how far I am going to go today." So I hauled him for a ways, and about five miles from the finish line I stopped and went to put him back in the lead. While I was working at putting him back, those four dogs of Cue Bifelt were acting like they never ran at all that day. They were standing there just yelling to go.

When I put Tennessee back in lead, he knew how far we had to go. And he knew what I wanted. So he just gave me everything he had for the last five miles and brought me back into town like there was nothing wrong with him. He was running on his own mind. He was a strange one. I don't know why this was, but a few weeks after Rendezvous, he was all right, and then he just died.

Anyway, I don't remember the last year Jimmy Huntington ran, but that last time he made a clean sweep of the Anchorage and Fairbanks races. And he was using Cue Bifelt's four dogs. When Bergman Sam won the North American in Fairbanks, he used those four dogs. When Cue won the Anchorage Rendezvous and the North American, he had those four dogs in his team. And when I won the Rendezvous there in Anchorage in 1958, I had Tennessee and those same four dogs.

I missed 1959, 1960 and 1961. I tried out a lot of dogs, but by then some other guys were racing too, like Bobby and Warner Vent, Bergman Sam and Cue Bifelt. We were actually producing too many mushers for the number of good dogs. I would try out what I could get my hands on, and then if they didn't look like a winning team to me and I couldn't talk fast enough to talk the next guy out of his good dogs, then I just turned my dogs over to whoever was coming in. So for three years there I missed.

Then in 1962 I had another of those outstanding teams, although all the dogs I had in 1958 were pretty well gone. Cue Bifelt and Bergman Sam were coming into Anchorage that year too, so I just got 11 dogs out of Huslia. But just looking at Cue's and Berman's teams, and with what I had learned about dogs by then, those 11 dogs looked really outstanding. For leaders I had Nellie, which is a famous dog today, and Tuffy, which was another famous leader, so I had a terrific team.

I would have come into Anchorage with those 11, but I really wanted to get some more. When I was in Huslia training, I heard that Bill Williams was in Hughes training a team. By then he was married to my sister, and my sister is bigger than he is. I figured that if he won't lend me his dogs, maybe my sister will shake him up. So on my way to Anchorage with my 11 dogs, I landed at Hughes. When I got there I went up to his house and had supper.

After supper I started asking him if I could use five dogs out of his team for the Anchorage race. He said, "No." He said that he wanted to race his dogs in the North American, and he wanted to save his dogs. I had a sponsor that winter. During the summer I had been a river pilot for Weaver Brothers, so they were sponsoring me for the race. But no one else had a sponsor, and they were going in on their own. So Bill Williams had me all worked up by then. He had 15 dogs at the time. I figured the guy must really have a good team of dogs if he had that much confidence in them to spend that kind of money to go into Fairbanks with them.

What I tried to do was just borrow the dogs, you know. I didn't talk any deals with him that were in his favor to start with. The way I figured it, everything was going to come my way. But I found out after a couple of hours of talking that here was a guy who was just as stubborn as I was. I had to change my way of talking to him then. So I told him that if he would lend me five dogs for the Rendezvous, I would lend him my 11 for the North American.

This team that Bill had was made up of his own dogs and William Koyukuk's dogs. So there was two people involved. What Bill said was, "It is okay with me. Go over and see William." Good thing the two had their cabins right next to each other.

So I went to see William and ask him if I could use the dogs. And William said, "Well, I got nothing to do with them. Billy borrowed the dogs from me. It is okay with me. Go over and ask Billy."

And then Billy would say the same thing over again.

And I would go back to William and tell him what Billy told me.

I kept walking back and forth between their two cabins, waking them up, until about five o'clock in the morning. I nearly gave up.

Then about five o'clock Billy got mad at me and told me, "Go ahead and take the five dogs. I am the one that is training the dogs, and if I say it is okay, then it is okay."

It took a lot of walking back and forth and a lot of talking to get those five dogs!

Anyway, those five dogs that I got from Bill Williams were really perfectly trained dogs. As far as borrowing dogs goes, those were the best trained dogs I ever got. They responded perfectly to every command. I never had any trouble with them whatsoever. I only got them a week before the Rendezvous and only put two drives on them before the race, but I ran all five of them all three days. That is an unusual thing. I haven't been able to do it since. Any dogs I have ever gotten from Bill Williams since were always well trained dogs. Anyway, I had a good race with those dogs. (They won the Rendezvous. Ed.) And Bill Williams got to run them in the North American. I think he came in third that year. So that was another outstanding dog team.

I sold my whole team after the '62 season. That was the team Keith Bryar ran after that.

Between 1963 and 1965 I never really got left behind when I raced. I think I was fifth or better all the time. But then I was just barely hanging on in there. It was hard racing. The dogs were not that good, just tough. It was a struggle. Let me tell you a little bit. I used to borrow dogs all the time, you know. I'd have the dogs all winter training them. Then say like Anchorage would be my first race. I'd run those dogs and prove how good they were and come in the money. The guys I borrowed the dogs from would come into town and when I'd make a good showing I'd wake up the next morning and find I got no dog team. The team was sold without my knowing it. I had a truck that I borrowed and I had people just come and claim dogs off the truck. I'd wind up with maybe 10 of my scrubs tied onto the truck. Man, that really hurt. That soured me. '65 was the last time I borrowed dogs.

In 1966 I didn't race at all.

My team started picking up again the fall of 1966. That's the year Penney's said they would sponsor me. I decided that if I want to go, I want to go on my own — own my own dog team. I really went into debt that year, really went into hock. Everything I earned that year, my whole summer's work, went into dogs. And all my living expenses from October on — I charged everything. Penney's sent a supply of dog food to Huslia by mail in the fall. Bob Grier, the manager of Penney's, said afterwards that if they ever sent food again, they were going to do it before the river froze so they could send it by boat. Cheaper. Penney's was a big help; they took a load off.

And I did come up with a pretty good dog team. That was the year of the big race; remember, the Centennial Iditarod Race? I made money that year. I mean, I paid for all my dogs and I paid all my bills. I was fifth in the Centennial race and sixth in the Rendezvous and third at Fairbanks. I was ready to go in debt again for next winter.

My team didn't improve that much from '67 to '68. But '68 was a tough race in Anchorage. It was hot. The trail was sloppy. Those dogs I had were not really fast dogs, but they were tough, steady dogs. They could run all day. My leaders were Blue and Rex and Coolie. I still got all three of them, my three old dogs. (George won the Rendezvous in '68. Ed.)

In 1969 my team had speeded up and Blue couldn't keep

George with Mr. and Mrs. Grier of Penney's, Anchorage Rendezvous, 1969. "Those people were sure nice to me." (photo by Maxine Vehlow)

Rendezvous, 1969. Looking at the picture from left to right, Johnny and Blue are in lead. "For commands, I would take Johnny over any other dog I have ever owned." "Blue was never the fastest dog in the world, but for honesty you couldn't ask for a better dog." In first swing, Coolie and Jarvi. In second swing, Chris and Yukon. In wheel, Ring and Stan. "Two of my better wheels dogs."
(photographer unknown)

1970 North American in Fairbanks. From left to right in lead, Scotty and Jarvi. In swing, Coolie and Chris. (photo by Nelson's Studio, Fairbanks)

1971 North American. Left to right in lead, Jarvi and Tex. In swing, Scotty and Lingo. (photo by Nelson's Studio)

up. So the first day I put her back in the team anyway and put Coolie and Johnny up front. And that damn Coolie bolted on me. Remember where the Muldoon crossing used to be? He bolted into a trailer court there after a loose dog. This was just the first six miles and I had 16 dogs and I couldn't stop them. There were a bunch of people on the track and I was yelling, wanting help from the crowd. And those sons of guns just stood there. And then this one girl came out and grabbed my sled and the dogs started dragging her. They were dragging me, and then they were dragging her too. When those guys saw the dogs dragging that girl, then they came out and helped me. But that was the race I lost by nine seconds.

The last two days I put Blue out there and I had no problems. I won the second heat easy. I lost that race the first six miles where they bolted. God dang, Blue could have

After the 1972 North American Championship. The trophy is being presented by Lieutenant Governor Red Boucher.

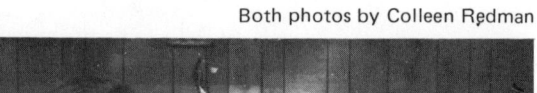

Both photos by Colleen Redman

"The Competition," Gareth Wright, three time winner of the Rendezvous, shown here in the 1972 North American where he finished second. The leaders belong to Bill Taylor, with Tanana Alice on the left. (photo by Nelson's Studio)

"The Competition," Bill Taylor, shown running in 1970, won the North American in 1968. From left to right in lead, Tanana Alice and Patches.
(photo by Nelson's Studio)

won that race for me; but I thought she wasn't fast enough. She wasn't fast, but she was honest.

In 1970 everything was fine until that last day right at the end. I lost that one by 30 seconds.

In 1971 I had a good dog team, you know. Just for a pair of leaders. What happened was that one of my leaders got in a dog fight and the other got stove up at Kenai. I had nothing left. Two weeks before Rendezvous I started calling around to see if I could rent a leader. McLean in Fairbanks loaned me Foxie. That guy really helped me out. If it wasn't for him I wouldn't have gotten out of town. I got Foxie 11 o'clock the night before the race and put him in lead. He did a good job, but the dog was a stranger to me.

Never in my life have I changed leaders around like I did that race. Five different leaders the first day, two the second day and three the third. I don't mind those kind of problems. They are my own problems. But when someone else louses it up for you ....

(George's Fairbanks record in recent years is: 1968, 4th; 1969, 1st; 1970, 1st; 1971, 2nd; 1972, 1st. Ed.)

A few years ago when snowgos came out, people lost interest in their dogs. This new thing came along, and everybody just abandoned their dogs and took to snowgoing. There are hardly any dogs up there in Huslia now. The population of dogs has gone down to nothing compared to what there used to be. Maybe there used to be 30 dog teams here 10 years ago. Now a couple of families, like the Sam family, have a twelve dog team. And Cue Bifelt has a few dogs. And I have my team.

But I think from what I've seen up in that area, in Allakaket and Hughes and anywhere along the Yukon River there — Tanana, Galena, Ruby, Nulato and those villages — that they may be coming back into dogs. They are not coming back into them for working or anything, they still got their snowgos, but they find that they can still have their dog teams to race at the same expense that they used to have them a long time ago. So I believe that there actually may be more local racing teams up there in the future.

But anyway, I will get on with your questions here.

TRAINING PHILOSOPHY

I think this book is just about everything I know about training and racing sled dogs. You hear a lot of comments about never believe a dog musher. Well, there is always a lot of kidding going on back and forth, like up in Tanana when a whole bunch of mushers get together. I guess you know how that is. But in these tapes I am telling you everything I have learned in a lot of years.

One thing I want to get across in this book is that I don't claim to know everything about dog mushing. I am just answering these questions by the way I do things. I don't claim that my way is the best for anybody else. If somebody wants to do something the way I do it, sure, that's okay, but he's on his own. I don't want him coming back and holding me responsible for anything that goes wrong.

Another point I want to get across is that the dog never makes a mistake. He is just a dog, and he does what he does because he is a dog and thinks like a dog. It is you that makes the mistake because you haven't trained him to do what you want him to do when you want him to do it. Or you have misjudged what he is able to do, physically or mentally. So if a mistake is made in that team, it is you that has made it, not the dog.

And about whipping. When you just mention the word "whipping" a lot of people think you are going to take the hide off that dog. I am not mad when I whip a dog, I am just training him. I use a whip to save my hand. I use a six foot whip and double it up so it can't hurt the dog. I don't whip hard. I only use it to where the dog thinks I am mad because he has not done what I asked him to. It is just like a spanking. The idea is, "I asked you to do something and you knew what you were supposed to do and you didn't do it, so this is what you are going to get." That is the message to get across to him. You don't have to kill somebody to get that message across.

I first learned how to mush dogs by watching my father, although I didn't realize it at the time. I was just a kid when he was doing it, and I never paid too much attention. If he told me to do something, I was just like any other kid. I'd just say to myself, "Well, what does he know?"

I was pretty small when I first raced. Maybe somewhere around eight years old. The first race I remember was a three dog race. I think it was shorter than three miles, more like a mile and a half. I remember the first time I raced in the seniors, after I came back from the hospital. I had most of my father's dogs. I just had one or two of my own. He started to tell my how to race these dogs, and I thought, "What the hell does he know about it? I am the one who is racing the dogs." Well, in that race by the time I found out that he knew what he was talking about, it was too late. Peter Wholecheese won that race and Jimmy Huntington was second and George Frank was third. I was seventh out of ten teams.

I don't think there is any difference between the way my father trained dogs and the way I do it now. Honestly, I think that if a guy is going to train dogs right, there is only one way he is going to do it.

You don't learn this game overnight. Some of the finer

points come with experiences you have on the trail, and some you can pick up from what has happened to other people. In that I think I've got an advantage over a lot of mushers. Where I come from almost everyone is a dog musher, or was a dog musher. You never know where a good idea is going to come from. You might think to yourself that this guy don't know nothing, but if you just sit and listen for a while, you might find that you pick up something that you didn't know.

When I am training dogs up in Huslia, I will ask anybody if they have seen a certain thing and what did they do about it. Then I sit back and listen. If I don't get an answer one place, I can always go to the next guy. Let's say I got all kinds of teachers up there in the villages. I've learned a lot from those guys. I never did tell anybody I learned something from them, but just by letting people talk and listening to them, a person picks up a lot of information, especially when you got a lot of mushers around. It doesn't make any difference what your opinion of the next guy is, he is going to come out with something that you don't know. Usually it is the little things that you pick up. Maybe, as a dog musher, basically you know all about it. But you could still pick up a lot of little tips here and there. At least that is the way I look at it.

Sled dog racing I don't think is any secret. It is just getting good dogs and training them properly. This dog mushing is sort of a religion. You have to be pretty dedicated. If you slack up a little bit, pretty soon you fall down in the last seconds. Maybe you lost that second two weeks before the race when you didn't really stick with it.

It is really hard to get around to start answering these questions on a tape recorder. You know, it is hard to sit around and talk to yourself.

FALL TRAINING SCHEDULE

October 10th
    Start training: Two miles with cart, four miles on snow.
    Use mostly year-old dogs; some older ones.
    Use team of eight dogs.

October 25th
    Runs up to eight miles.
    No obedience training; just toughening.
    Run four or five times a week.

November 1st
    Use 10 dog string.
    Forty minute runs; still toughening.

November 15th
    Run every other day.
    Still toughening.
    Go 10 miles fast.
    By end of November go 10 miles wide open.

December 1st
    Start training dogs to obey commands.
    Run 12 dog string.

Go 12 miles.

December 15th

Run three or four times a week.

Run wide open all the time.

Work up to 20 mile test at the end of December.

October 10th

I start training in the fall by the temperature and the snow on the ground. Some years I do some cart training, but this road we got here is sometimes nothing but dust. Like this year, I didn't do any cart training because it was just too much dust on that road, and I didn't think it would pay off. If I do any cart training, it is usually the younger dogs, the pups that are getting the training. I rarely monkey with the older dogs before snow. Most of the time we get our snow by October 10th, and so that is when I start my training.

Right now I am starting out with 38 dogs. All I can afford to keep is 24 or 25, so I am going to try to sell some of them. I never sell a bum dog. It is more important to me to keep up my reputation than it is to make a quick buck. I'll make more money in the long run anyhow by selling only good dogs. Naturally I am going to try to keep the best dogs for myself, at least for one season. But any grown dog I sell is a good dog, or I wouldn't sell it.

Out of the 24 or 25 that I keep, three or four go lame over the winter, especially in the races. Then when I do get them in a race, I find that there are a couple that might be lacking in speed.

In October I'm running small strings, only eight dogs. I'm mostly running the younger dogs, dogs that are going on their first year. Some of the older ones I hook up, and some of them I don't.

My first runs are just about two miles if I use a cart. If I start with a sled, I go about four miles. They are not fast runs either. They are run at the dogs' own pace. Actually I am stopping a lot. I try to keep them running just by liking it.

What I try to do right from the start is to train these dogs to run all the time. When I start training in the fall and go real short miles, the team always starts out real fast. While they are still going good, before any dog breaks into a trot, I stop. When I take off again they are going wide open. I am building the team up to go further. When they are in shape, I step up the distance. Like if I start at two miles I maybe go from two miles to four miles when I know they could take four miles. If say I start at four miles, I stop every mile for that four miles. A dog, even after he went say three and a half miles and I stop, he is going to start running again when I pull that hook out. After a while he is tough enough so that he can go that four miles wide open. Then I step them up a little more, always going at this pace.

When I keep doing this, these dogs are learning how to lope fast. It is being built into them. I set this pace in my dog team early in the fall. They are really eager then and doing it on their own. Pretty soon to them it is a natural gait. It just comes to them that this is the slowest they are going to go.

I couldn't always get away with this because sometimes there is a whole pile of snow and all they are doing is trotting. But then I don't say nothing either. I don't ask for any more because this is all my dogs can do.

I set this pace where I figure this is going to be their slow speed in a race. A nice, easy, long lope is all it is. I really couldn't say how fast this pace is, but it is fast, something like 14 or 15 miles an hour. When I am entering a race, I always figure this is the slow speed, and from there they are going to go faster and faster, just like shifting gears. There is just one top speed that my dogs have that I don't hit very often. Maybe even when I am winning a race I don't hit this top speed even once. I've done this before and still come out a winner because of the basic pace these dogs have got.

October 25th

If I train steady, I'd say by October 25th I'll have them probably up to eight miles. This is still pretty much on their own. I never do any obedience training right now, like whipping or anything of that sort. October is just a toughening in period, and all I am doing is just working them. I run them about five times a week because it is just slow runs and they are taking it easy.

Some of the younger dogs that are just goofing off and don't look like they will make it, I just go ahead and shoot those dogs right now. (Since food is at a premium in the villages, dogs which do not fulfill a purpose must be shot. Ed.)

I think I will tell you here how I hook up my team. Usually when I am training up here by myself I am pretty much doing it all alone. So what I do is I have a long chain that I string pretty close to where my towline runs. I get my dogs put into harness and snap them on to this long chain. This way I don't get very far away from the dogs as I am hooking them up. I can keep an eye on them and get to them really fast if they are chewing the line or something. I never whip them for chewing on anything, maybe just a little slap is all.

The best way actually to hook up a team is to start from the back end, except for line-biters. I have my towline tied up front so I can work from the back to the front. I hook my leaders up last. When I get the leaders hooked up, I undo the front of the towline and go back to the sled, before the leaders turn around and come back to me. Usually it is the young leaders that will do that.

November 1st

I have started them with a two or a four mile run and kept stepping it up. I have been saying the number of miles all along here just to give you an idea. I have really been guessing at the distance. I expect my mile in Huslia is a little bit more stretched out than one in Anchorage. So if you start to add up how far I go and how fast and how long it takes me and the dates, it just isn't going to work out.

Actually what I do is run by time. I have a good stop watch so I can be accurate about times. Maybe I step my time up ten minutes every two weeks. By November 1st I've got them up to 40 minute runs, and this is not wide open either. They are still just toughening in. From November I'm running a 10 dog string. Usually I've got a little weight on the sled, maybe 10 pounds over what I will be hauling in a race.

A dog that just isn't going fast enough and is working too hard sometimes just can't seem to keep his body straight and pulls off to one side. Like maybe his front end will go to the right and his rear end will go to the left. A dog that pulls to one side like this picks it up when he is a pup. This is one reason that when you first hook a pup up, you have to work him one side for a little ways and then switch him over to the other side to teach him to work on both sides. As soon as a person first notices a pup working too hard and pulling off to one side, he should switch this dog to the other side, even if the dog doesn't want to go on the other side.

If the dog that is pulling off is running single lead, if you could take enough weight off his backline, then he should start running straight. I find that with these dogs when you really wind them up, they will straighten out and start working perfectly.

This dog that bears to the left on his rear end and to the right on his front end should be running on the right side. Now over the past years I used to think that I would get more speed out of him on the left side. But a dog like this, when you are hitting your top speed, he is actually better off on the right side. You could get more speed out of him and better pulling power, better work. It took me a long time to pick this up. I just picked it up the last few years.

November 15th

Starting from November 15th I run them every other day. By now I have them up to a 10 mile run that they are loping pretty strong on their own. Then from about November 15th I start making them run this 10 miles fast. By the end of November I got them to where they can go 10 miles wide open.

December 1st

By the first of December I'm running a 12 dog string. I start stepping up my miles a little bit more. Maybe I start going a 12 mile run.

December 1st I start training the dogs to respond to my commands.

My commands are always to speed up. I never have no commands to slow down. All I am teaching the team to do is go one way, and that is forward. I never teach my dogs to stop. When you are in heavy training your dogs will stop when you say "whoa." They want to stop so you don't have to teach them. You have to teach them to go forward. I try to say as few words as possible. I don't think you have to have a whole bunch of words. When I use that "Get up!" they gotta go then. That's the only command you need.

All fall when I am out with the team, the younger dogs are picking up a lot of things like the sounds I make when I'm driving the older dogs. When I holler "Get up!" at the older dogs, they will pick it up and the younger ones will have to pick it up, too. After a while it gets so the young ones will respond every time I give that command.

The main thing is to get the dogs to respond when you ask them to do something. You have got to get that message across. Every time you ask for something, they got to give it to you. If they don't, they have to be corrected. There is only one way for me to correct, and that is with the whip. I pretty much train in a wooded area here in Huslia where I could stop any time I want to. It is like having perfect control over the team all the time.

I never pop my whip right on my dog. If you pop it just right, you have a good chance of splitting that dog's hide wide open. What I do is I double it up. When you double it up and just hit the dog, then there is no chance of really hurting that dog. I don't whip hard. The idea is that you didn't do what I told you to, so this is what you are going to get. It is just the same thing as a spanking. You don't have to kill somebody to get the message across. Starting about December 1st, if I tell the dogs to pick it up and they don't pick it up — some of them will, and some of them won't — then that is when I get on them. When I ask my dogs to pick it up, that is not the word I am using. The command is "Get up!"

Say I got a 12 dog team and am going on a 12 mile run. I got one dog in there that starts slopping off at 10 miles. I call him to pick it up, and he doesn't pick it up. I call him again, and he doesn't pick it up. Well, I got to teach this dog to pick it up when I call him. Say his name is Rex. When I say, "Get up, Rex!" if he don't get with it, I would whip him to make him pick it up. When I whip him he learns he is supposed to give it to me. I have taught him a lesson. So he would pick it up for a mile and maybe I would let him go for that day.

The next time he slacks off again at 10 miles, I would whip him. If he slacks off a mile after that, I would whip him again. As long as I know that this dog has got it, I am going to keep working on him until he gives it to me every time I say to pick it up. As long as I know he has got it, I am going to get it. Say I did this for 10 days straight. Well, by then I am getting pretty tired of it. After 10 days I am either going to make that dog or I am going to forget him.

When I have been saying whip a dog, I didn't mean to really work him over. Like I say, I double my whip up so I can't really hurt the dog with it. All I am trying to do is just get the message across that I am mad. That don't take much of a whipping. But after this 10 days straight of whipping, on the 10th day I really work this dog over. I really whip him. Today he is either going to do it, or I am going to forget him. Every time I have done this, I find that this dog will really turn on for me. Every time I say something, he is with it. He is always right there giving me everything he's got.

When I am training my dogs and I come to a hill, I want my dogs to lope up that hill and not quit on me. I know they can do it. When I am half way up and they slow down to a trot, if I tell them to "Get up" and they just won't give it to me, then that is another time I would whip them.

A fast trotter ought to go from a trot into a lope if he is properly trained. I figure that a dog that can trot fast can lope faster. There are dogs that are just trotters and are stubborn and hard to take from a trot to a lope. The only answer then is whipping. At least this is the way I do it. When your dogs are pooped though, then the only way you could make them pick it up is by pedaling. Naturally when you are pedaling your dogs can speed up more. This would take the trotter out of his trot.

It sounds like I am forever whipping my dogs. Well, this is not the case. Actually, in the last two years I haven't had to do this much because I haven't had that many dogs that were untrained. The trained dogs will teach the untrained ones to pick it up. I've had some dogs that don't need no whipping at all. They just picked up from the other dogs what they were supposed to do. Some dogs I have been running year after year and never had to touch them, and I have gotten everything I can out of them. Everything they had to give me. I don't really like to whip a dog. One time this winter I thought about it for almost two weeks before I went out and whipped this one dog.

You never want to whip your dogs in their lot or behind the barn. It is always on the trail when they didn't pick it up when you told them to. You have got to catch them right in the act. When you ask for something and they don't give it to you is the only time. You don't go and just whip them for nothing. I think the dog should be right in the team when you whip him. I don't think you should take the time out to unhook him. Usually I tell my dogs "easy" when I go out to whip one dog. I never want my dogs so scared of a whip that they are jumping all over. Usually when I go out to whip one dog, the whole team lies down right on the trail.

When I am whipping a dog I have the whip doubled up and I am carrying the jingler in the same hand. If the dog hears the jingler at the same time as the whip comes down on him, naturally the whip and the jingler are just one thing to him. The reason I do this is because I don't want to have to be swinging that whip in a race. I want the sound of the jinglers to be enough.

When I am whipping a dog, my voice is saying that this is the way it is going to be and there is no other way around it. I use this mean tone of voice like, "You do this or else you are going to get this whip on you." The whip is backing up my tone of voice, and the jingler is there too. The whipping and the jingler and the tone of your voice all go together.

When I holler "Get up!" it can have three different meanings. It all depends on what tone I am using. If I holler "Get up!" easy, then I just want a little from them. If I holler "Get up!" a little harder then I want more. But if I holler "Get up!" like I was mad at them, then I am after fear because maybe they are tired of going at their top speed, but I know I have got to have a little more. Then I use the tone of voice that I use when I am whipping them. That is one of the big things, how you use your tone of voice.

When I am training a team I am all business. I am training to win. Whether I win or not, I am training my dogs to listen to me and give me what I ask them to give me.

If you could just keep your cool, even when you are mad, if you don't just blow up, then you are in good shape. That is one of the main things. If you could just never lose control of your temper. That could run away with you pretty fast. And when you do that, you are goofing up your whole training program. If you want to be a good dog musher, you keep your temper around your dogs. Maybe you couldn't do it in a barroom, but by God, when you are around your dog team, you keep your temper to yourself.

December 15th

The last two weeks of December I probably run my dogs, oh, three or four times a week. This is every other day. From December 15th on they are learning to run wide open. There is no such thing as slowing down for these dogs, they are setting a pretty fast pace when they are just running on their own. Every time your dogs run on their own, you want to make sure it is at that good basic pace — maybe 15

"But if I holler 'Get up!' like I was mad at them..." Rendezvous 1969.

(photo by Maxine Vehlow)

Huslia
Dec. 14 – 70

Dear Bella
 I am glad you like the tape. I don't know what they will look like when it is written up. We can put more in I think once we know what I said. I don't remember what I taped now. Dog are going good. I got them running 16 miles only we got to much snow.
The moose are staying on the trail which makes for a lot of holes on the trail. Might hurt some dogs. Hope not,
my leaders about got a moose the other day. I don't think they were 20 feet from the moose when he got off the trail. He was trying to out run the dogs on the trail.
 by now
 Sincerely
 George

miles an hour. You have been building toward this all fall as you were training. After December they should be just clipping this off with no trouble at all. It is just their natural run. When you got this pace, then there is only one way to go, and that is faster. When you tell them to pick it up from that pace, you make sure they pick it up, even if you have to pedal yourself to speed them up.

I step up their miles until I get in about three 20 mile runs. By the end of December what I am shooting for is a 20 mile run wide open, just as fast as the dogs can run. In other words, by the end of December I will be ready for any race.

At the end of December I give my dogs what I call a test. I have been working up to this test for two and a half months. I've got my 20 mile course that has been measured by snow travelers. I run this for four days straight. When I am giving this test, the first day maybe all my dogs go good. They make a good run. The next day maybe one dog in there wants to quit at 15 miles and I have to whip him to get him going again. He will probably try the same thing the next day, and I whip him again. By the fourth day he won't try it again. In a race like the Rendezvous, this same dog won't quit on me, but he will show signs of wanting to quit at say the 20 mile point in the race.

The only reason I take them for those 20 mile runs at the end of December is to see how tough they are and how much pressure they can take. By pressure I mean I make them do the 20 the best they could. Last winter I had a team that would do the course in an hour and ten minutes for four days straight. That was in '69.

This 20 mile course is the longest run I give my dogs. Way back in '62 I never made a run that was less than 20 miles. Sometimes I used to run the dogs 40 miles. I used to start my training then about the first of January, and most of my dogs were borrowed dogs. What happens when you train a dog this far every other day for a month is pretty soon that dog gets to thinking, "Well, I am going for a 40 mile run." And he runs like he is going for 40 miles. He is pacing himself for 40 miles so he could finish the run, and it has got to be a slower pace than if he is going for just 20 miles.

Now I start training short miles and step them up. Then in January I cut back again. I try to keep the dogs off balance. They never know how far they are going today, whether it will be 10 miles or 20 miles. This way I am the one who is setting the pace of the team. But if I went on a 30 mile run every day, then they are the ones who would be setting the pace. The training is the same on responding and everything, but the dogs pace themselves differently. A 40 mile pace today could be too slow. I hear there are people still doing it though. In a tough, 25 mile race they might come close to winning today, but I doubt if they could actually win it.

At 20 miles my dogs have a pace set for any race. I have a chance of winning anything from a 16 mile race on up. There are teams up here in Alaska that would go for 15 miles at a better clip than my team could go, but you get them to go any further than that and you would find that my team — if they were a top team like I had last year — should come out ahead. I don't think my team would be able to win a 10 mile race, but when it gets beat, it won't be by very much. The poorest I ever did in any of the preliminaries — 12, 14, and 16 mile races — was fourth. And when I did fourth, I was never very far behind. I have won some of the preliminary races, too.

So actually this training method could work for any distance race. The reason it is going to work is because these dogs, at the pace that I've taught them to set, just at their natural pace that was trained into them, are actually going pretty fast.

WINTER TRAINING

After January 1st the team is trained. My dogs don't need no more whipping. I got them trained to my tone of voice by then. I could either just talk to them nice and they would run, or I could use a tone that sounds like I mean it, and they will know what I am talking about. I cut back on their miles, and I don't take them out as often. I use attitude runs then.

Let's say, for instance, that I had a 20 mile race two weeks after I did that test of 20 miles for four days straight. When I did that test, I took quite a bit of life out of the dogs. They are tired and tired of running. They are going to need rest. So I take them on just five or six mile runs for two weeks, say three times a week. By the time I hit this 20 mile race, they should be eager and willing to run again. If everything is with me, my dogs should be in top shape for this race.

The races that are run in Anchorage every Sunday in January are the preliminary races. They have the 10, 12, 14 and 16 mile preliminaries. If I race in any of these preliminaries, I run two short training runs of maybe 10 miles each week besides whatever preliminary race I am running. If a dog is going to race every weekend, whether it is Saturday and Sunday or just Sunday, he should only be run twice during the week, providing he is already in condition. If you have to condition him more, he would need probably one more day. But add any more days than that and you are asking too much of the dog.

Mostly what I am working on at this time is to get a little life back in the team after all the hard training of the last couple of months. On runs like this I stop and pet the dogs quite a bit to make them happy. And sometimes I take a rider in the basket more or less for company for me. I am trying to build the dogs' morale back up and just keep them in shape. Once they are in shape, it doesn't really take that much running. It is mostly just staying up to where you want them to stay. You don't want them to get soft on you, and yet you don't want to run them so much that they go sour on you.

I don't like to race my dogs every week in the preliminary races. I have a 24 dog team — give or take a dog — and I try to run 12 dogs one weekend and the other 12 the next weekend. I have raced two teams on one weekend when I let my handler race one team and I raced the other. But I don't recommend that either. The handler might not run the dogs properly, and if a dog got hurt, I would be mighty unhappy. Whichever team I am running, it is sort of like checking them out. I want to see how they act under certain conditions. All I am doing in the preliminary race is just getting ready for the big race. I want to see how the dogs run under pressure, but I don't want to do it every weekend.

The main thing I always have on my mind when I am training is the Rendezvous. But then I have the Kenai-Soldotna State Championship in mind, too. I usually got a pretty lousy bunch of dogs before I hit the State Championship. They are as tough as they are ever going to be physically, and they are trained to respond when I tell them something, but after all that hard running, mentally they just aren't with it. The hard training takes something out of the mind. So I keep building their morale up and trying to get some life back into them. I try to bring them up to their peak for the State Championship.

I lay my team off one day after Kenai, or any big race, and then take them for a three or four mile run. This is not a real run then either. The dogs are just sort of taking it easy. I do this with a six dog or smaller team. If it is any bigger, I usually have to holler at somebody for going at a trot. I am just checking out any stiffness and just sort of checking the team over. So they get one day off, and then they get a checkup.

Then after that, I try to put some life into them again for the Rendezvous, which is two weeks later. I want to have my dogs in top shape for this race. About a week before the Rendezvous I am going on 10 mile runs.

I run my dogs three and two days before the Rendezvous. Well, these last two runs I take my whip out and go through the whole team just sort of swinging it back and forth on them, but not really whipping them. Maybe they haven't seen that whip for a month, and this is just to remind them that it is still there. This is one thing that is really important. I've found that in the past I've made a mistake. I just built towards attitude after I got through training and never did remind them that the whip was there. In a tough race like the Rendezvous, a lot of places you have to use force just to keep going.

I have had four months to get ready for this race. My dogs are as tough as they are ever going to be, and I know just how tough that is. I know how far my dogs can run and what they are going to do when I ask for more. No matter what kind of commands I give them, I know what they are going to give me. I have put them through all kinds of pressure. I know everything there is to know about these dogs. At least this is the frame of mind I am in when I hit that race. We all make mistakes, but they won't be too big ones.

These dogs are at their peak. They are really ready to go. I take that whip out and show it to them, wanting their nerves to be right up on edge. I want to have myself honed up for that race, too. I want my team and me thinking just the same thing, thinking nothing but win.

If you use this training method, your dogs should be right on edge. They should be peaked out. They may not win the race, but they will give you the best they have got.

Well, that is the way it should be, but it don't always work out that way. Like this winter, I really had a bad training winter. The dog team was there to do it, but the weather was not with me. There were stretches when it was so cold I had to tie them up for two weeks and never run. Then maybe it would warm up and I would run them for a couple of days. Then it would start snowing so much that when I could get out I was just plowing snow all the time. This was the winter of 1971.

When I came to Anchorage three weeks before Rendezvous, my dogs hadn't been out for two weeks up there in Huslia. When I got on the plane up there, it was something like 50 below. I still knew when I loaded the dogs that I had the dog team that could win, but I knew their training was not with them. Another thing I knew was that if I really got with it when I got down to Anchorage, and if the weather was right, I could get the best those dogs got. They were outstanding dogs, so I knew I would come in third or better. This I knew from past experience. So when I loaded my dogs up there it was something like 50 below, and when I got to Anchorage it was something like 20 above. That was 70 degrees difference in the weather; something I didn't count on.

The temperature didn't seem to affect them right at first, but then I started running them. This was six days before the State Championship, so I started running them every day right up until the race. I got in that race down at Kenai, and I knew I wasn't ready. But then again I thought "I will just ride this race out and see how I finish." That put eight days of steady running on my dogs. I came in second in Kenai, and that really surprised me. I had thought I would finish further back. But I did hurt the most important dog in my team, my best command leader.

So after the race, the change of weather and then that eight days of hard running got to the dogs. They quit eating. Change of weather always does that to dogs. When it is cold, they are feeling good. You go out in your yard and they want to run. Then all of a sudden the weather breaks and it warms up, and that warm weather drags the team down. They don't feel like running. They don't feel like doing nothing. This winter coming from cold to warm had more effect on my dogs because I was putting them under a lot of strain at the same time as they were feeling this weather. When they quit eating, I just had to lay the team off completely for a while. They were eating snow and I couldn't make them drink their water. That was one of the things that was really getting to me. I would run them to the vet, and there would be nothing actually wrong with them. They didn't have a virus of any kind. It was just the weather and the strain getting to them.

Anyway, I came in second in the Rendezvous. Coming in second surprised me, too. Just goes to show you that you can't keep a good dog down. He'll go down all right, but if you have the right training on him as far as commands go whether he is feeling his best or not, he is going to give you the best performance that he possibly could.

QUESTIONS AND ANSWERS

George being congratulated by a fan after winning the 1972 North American at Fairbanks.
Photo by Colleen Redman

BREEDING

Could you tell us anything about your father's breeding program?

I think the breeding has gone back and forth a lot, like say between the villages on the Yukon – Nulato and Koyukuk and Galena. In those days, according to what I heard, a lot of dogs were being traded back and forth.

Probably the best team my father ever owned came from when he got a female from a guy down in Nulato, George Ismalka. He bought a female off him. The best bunch of pups my folks ever raised was from that bitch. When my father had that breed and they were racing up there, he used to win all the races.

My dad and Bergman Sam's dad were really great friends all their lives. They were great White Mule makers too. They used to get drunk together out in camp all the time. According to what my older brother tells me, Sammy Sam would try to get this dog – this dog's name was Tootsie – from my father. And my dad wouldn't let it go. Every time they drank together and had a party, Sammy would try to get Tootsie from my father. Well, he finally did manage to get the dog, and his family came up with a good team after that. For quite a few years nobody could beat Sammy after he got ahold of Tootsie and had some pups.

Even just lately the whole Sam's breeding is mostly from that Tootsie breed. And that came out of Nulato.

Does anyone in the village worry about pink pads or spotted tongues?

Well, my father always used to put down any puppies that were born with pink pads. When I get one with pink pads, I keep it and hope for the best.

Quite a few dogs around have spotted tongues. Johnny Allen in Ruby used to have a whole strain of spotted-tongue dogs, and they were good dogs.

Where do you get your best dogs?

Just talking about dogs generally, it seems like the breed in Huslia is, I don't know what it is, but they seem to be the most proven breed up here in the state of Alaska. The average production of good dogs in Huslia is much higher than any place I have been to. I have gone to a lot of places and gone through a lot of dogs, just buying dogs generally, but I still get my best percentage of dogs right in Huslia.

Hughes and Allakaket get a good percentage of dogs, too, when they raise a litter of pups. The breeding between those three villages has been pretty much passed back and forth. We have a lot of inbreeding up there today. There isn't very many dogs passing in and out of those villages except maybe for house dogs and maybe for some new dogs that I bring in. But then we don't want to do very much experimenting either. We don't breed dogs that we aren't sure of, that aren't already proven. We always stick with the local breed because they have proven themselves many times. I could buy a bunch of pups up there and always manage to come up with some really good dogs, no matter who I got those pups from.
What factors do you take into consideration when you are deciding which dog to mate with whom?

I have always taken the proven breed into consideration before I did anything. Proven stock are dogs that are well built and have made my team.

I got two females in my yard these last few years that I usually raise my pups from. They are Blue and Chris. Blue used to be a Simon dog that was a leader a few years back. I'm running a lot of her pups in my team right now. It seems like every litter of pups she has had, she has come up with damn near 100 percent good dogs. I have some other females that I have raised some pups from, and I have got some good dogs out of them too. But my main breeding females are Blue and Chris. I would say that the reason I breed those two is because they are both tough dogs and the breeding in their background is an old breed in Huslia. This strain has been producing I would say the best dogs around here for a long time.

I've got four different studs in my team, and one in

there seems to be an outstanding producer. The male I use is Coolie. He is 11 years old this winter. I ran him this winter, but I think he is just about at his limit now. But he is throwing a lot of good dogs for me. I got a lot of his pups in my team right now. Coolie originated from my father's dogs. The whole breeding went through the Sam family and is spread around pretty thick up there now. I have stuck with those two dogs because of all the good dogs their strains have produced up there in that area. You could see the two sides of the breeding. When you go up the Koyukuk to either Allakaket or Hughes or down the river to Huslia, these two strains are pretty much the same thing.

You take famous dogs like Nellie and Tuffy. I am sure from what I was told that they are from the same strain. All those dogs were either inbred or crossbred or line-bred, whatever you want to call it, at one time or another.

Once in a while I breed out, just to see how the pups will turn out. If they do turn out, I take them into my kennel too.

When a person starts to monkey around with a new strain, starts experimenting, then you are talking about a lot of money. If you got a proven strain, it is best to stay with that, as long as they are winning, instead of trying something else. If you start getting beat, then that is the time to start looking around for something else. As long as I am doing okay with what I got here, I would keep breeding just what I got. What I look for most is just the proven stock, just the proven strain of dogs. That is what makes me decide who to mate with who.

How many litters a year do you usually raise? Approximately how many pups out of these litters will end up on your team?

I raise from two to three litters a year, between 15 and 20 pups. I sell a lot of pups, you know, before I try them. I sell those on their breeding alone. Or I sell them right after I break them if they look good. The buyer always knows just what he is getting. Last year I raised 20 pups. I just broke them. I plan on keeping 10 of these pups and selling the other 10. I got 34 dogs and some of them are up in years. I got one there that's 10 years old and a few there that's six, and so I'm going to have to start adding some new young dogs in there this year.

Would you breed a dog that is a poor racing dog himself but comes from a good racing line?

Ya, I'd do that if I didn't have nothing else, provided the dogs have a background of coming from a line of good racing dogs. In fact, I have done it before and came up with some good pups. In a litter of five, I maybe came up with one really outstanding dog out of a breeding like this. But when I bred dogs like this, always the female was good and the other side was an accidental breeding. I really wouldn't go this route unless I didn't have no choice.

What breeding has gone into the making of the Indian Dog?

I was discussing that with Jimmy Huntington. It seems like nobody really knows where the Indian Dog came from.

Did any of the Seppala strain get into native breeds of Alaskan Dogs?

I really don't know about those Seppala dogs. I wouldn't know one if I saw one.

(One of the things that George often does during the summer is to fight forest fires for the Bureau of Land Management. He is so experienced that he is a supervisor.

During September of 1970 when forest fires raged through the state of Washington, the Bureau of Land Management sent crews of Alaskans to help out. One of these crews was from Huslia, with George in charge. This crew had a fire camp at Brief, in front of the home of Mr. and Mrs. Carl Zerrenner. When the Huslia crew finally stopped the fire at the edge of the Zerrenner's property, Mr. and Mrs. Zerrenner returned with their female Siberian, Nipper of Entiat, and her litter of puppies. Mr. and Mrs. Zerrenner say that the Huslia crew made a big fuss over all the dogs. The odd thing was that according to Frances Sinrud, the breeder of Nipper, she is one eighth Seppala and looks one hundred percent like the strain. So George did see as much of a Seppala-looking dog as is around today.

Another ironic thing is that as dog mushers themselves, Mr. and Mrs. Zerrenner didn't know in the confusion who it was that had saved their home. As much as they regret that they didn't know at the time that George Attla was there, at least they have and will always treasure the little sign, "Huslia," that the crew left behind. Ed.)

Do you think any kind of hound or Collie or Labrador is in your Huslia breed?

The only reason I know that there's Collies and Labradors and hound is because I've seen these Collies and Labradors and hound dogs in the village quite a few years back, so the breeding's gotta be here. There's no getting around that. Once in a while you get a throw back. You could see the hound in some of these dogs.

What do you think about these crosses?

I used to borrow different dogs from different people, and I've ran some of these crosses. They were good dogs. They were just as good as anything I had.

Do you know of any Siberian or Malamute in the Huslia breed?

I wouldn't know really, so I couldn't answer that question.

What do you know about the dogs from other villages? How are they different from Huslia Dogs?

Actually I haven't seen any difference in the dogs from the villages around Huslia. Right now I am working on a boat. I've started right from the mouth of the Yukon and I've stopped at every village on the way up. So far I'm at Anvik. This is still the lower Yukon. So far from what I've seen of these dogs on the lower Yukon, they look too big for racing. Another thing, it looks like there has been a lot of cross breeding here. There is a lot of hound type, big hound type, great big dogs. They are much bigger than anything we have in Huslia or that area.

Do you buy or raise most of your dogs? Which is better? Which is cheaper in the long run?

Which is cheaper? Well, I would say that you would come out about the same. I really can't say which the best is. I raise most of my dogs. Actually, if I don't raise them, it is someone else here in the village that raises them.

When I was looking over these questions this evening, particularly the one "Do I Raise Most of My Dogs," I started looking at my kennel and thinking. Looking at the breeding of those dogs, of the 38 dogs I have, 34 are local, Huslia breeding, and only four are a completely different strain. There are two from Tanana and two pups I got from Fairbanks last spring. So I stick pretty much to home-grown dogs. I know they are good. (The Tanana dogs made the team one season; the Fairbanks pups didn't make it at all. During the 1972 season George had a dog from Grayling on his team. Ed.)

Would you ever go back to a wolf strain to improve your breed?

I don't think I would. I have discussed this with Jimmy and Sidney Huntington and some old timers around here that have had some experience with wolf dogs. They just don't go for this wolf strain. They say that if you get too close to a wolf strain, you'd be coming up with quitters and dogs so stubborn that you couldn't handle them.

I have discussed this a lot of times with Larsen Charlie just over a cup of coffee at my house. Charlie used to work with the mail team up there in Huslia. He said that these dogs were really stubborn dogs. I don't remember exactly how much wolf his dogs had in them, but they were either half wolf or more. And according to what he told me, he said that early in the morning when they hooked the dogs up, that these wolf strain would really move. But once the sun came up, all through the day these dogs would be moving, but they would just be monekying around. You couldn't do nothing with them. They would lift their leg at every tree they felt like lifting a leg on, and stuff like this. But he said that once the sun started going down, there was no holding these dogs. It seemed like they were more night runners than day runners. There was just too much wolf in them.

PUPPIES

Do you have any special training for puppies before they are of running age?

When you are raising a litter of pups for dog racing, it's good to handle them when they are small. I don't know how young you could do this, but you have to make friends with them. Before they get too big you have to get across to them that the human race is a friend to them, that they don't have to be scared of you.

Some of my dogs are really too shy. Well, where this came from is that they were not handled when they were little. I never had enough time, and I had someone else taking care of them. All that person was paid to do was just feed and water and generally look after things. The guy didn't have enough interest in the dogs to go play with the pups. So because of that I have come up with dogs that I would have

George and friends behind his house.

a hard time handling.

So you get in a race and maybe you get in a great big tangle. Well, the friendly dogs are easy to untangle. They are not shying away from you. They are just standing there and waiting for you to undo this mess. Whereas a touchy dog, the one that was never handled as a pup, he is just wild. He is the hardest one to undo when he is in a mess.

You have to start them young to be able to do this. They are not spoiled or anything. They just know you are not there to harm them. They are easier to handle in harness then.

What is the best age to tell if a pup is well built?

I kind of wait on that until they are about seven months old. Then I can go by their build. But I couldn't tell before then.

Is this when you cull your litters?

No. I can pick them earlier than that, but I really don't go by their build.

Actually, the way I do it is like this. Most of my pups are born in late July or August. When I am training in the fall I let those pups run behind the sled. At three and a half or four months old you could tell which is the fastest pup when they are chasing you. They can't keep up with you, but the first puppy you meet up with on your way in you know is the fastest one. Even when they are a year old, this pup is still the fastest one in there. There is no getting around this. I always thought it would work out different, but the pup that is shown the fastest at four or five months is actually the fastest dog in the litter.

Out of a litter of five, you'd get two that's really fast, one that's kind of in the middle and then two that kind of get left behind all the time. At that age you could really get rid of the two slowest ones. But I never do. And I could say that I hardly ever came up with one of those slow ones that made it. With the cost of raising pups it's not worth while keeping the slowest ones. It would be best if you stuck with the fastest ones of the litter.

At what age and how do you start to train a pup?

I start training them mostly between three and four months old, running behind the sled. Not all of the pups want to go out all of the time, so the pups that don't want to go out, I put them in the sled and drop them off two or three miles out. I keep doing this and pretty soon they just automatically start following me out.

At about six months old I stop running them all of a sudden and keep them tied up for about a week. For the last couple of months they have been chasing the team, and when you keep them tied up and they see those dogs going out, they are just about tearing up the ground by the time you are ready to break them. So actually they don't know the feel of the harness until after the first couple of hundred yards, and usually they are with it by then.

When you first start running a pup in harness, what kind of team do you use?

I wouldn't hook up more than eight, which maybe sounds like a lot of dogs to some people, but I would hook up four trained dogs and four pups that I am breaking. When I do this I'm not going out for no speed run. You have to go slow.

I got those four adult dogs in front to keep that line held out, and I come along behind with the brake on. If I don't want to use the brake, I take a big load so that sled goes slow. So actually, those pups are on a really tight line. There is no jumping over their necklines because the front dogs are slacking or anything like that. Those leaders have got to go where you want them to go. You have got to be able to stop the team when you want so you can go out and pet the dogs or do whatever has to be done. You have got to have complete control over that team at all times, that's the main thing. There couldn't be any mess-up on that first hookup.

Do you keep a new pup in the same position, or do you change him around?

One of the things you want to do is keep switching the pups around. Like you have been working one on the left side and one on the right side. Say you take them on a mile training run. Say you switch them back and forth three times in that mile. If you don't do this, usually the side that the pup takes off from the yard on, that's the side he wants to run on. If you just kept him on that one side, you are going to have a hard time breaking him of running on that side. Where if you kept changing him back and forth, then naturally he learns to work on either side. That is one of the things you want to keep in mind. That is a big point in training pups.

Do you change your pup training program to suit one that appears to be different?

No, I train them just about the same way.

Some of the pups would be crazy to go. Others would be kind of touchy because they are scared of you. The pup that is touchy you got to be careful of. The main thing is to make sure you don't scare him any more. If you do, he might be so scared that when you get him in harness he will be looking back at you, and you wouldn't want that to happen. At least I wouldn't want it to happen. The pup that is giving you a bad time pulling you and jerking you around, what I do is just slap him a little bit to calm him down, just so I could handle him.

I don't hook up a whole bunch of lively pups and a whole bunch of pups that are scared of me separately. I run them together.

How many times would you run a pup in harness when he was not willing and caused trouble before you gave up on him?

Well, the reason he would do that would be because he really didn't know what you wanted. You have got to teach him what you want.

You might be able to keep stopping and petting him and just try to get him happy to where he wants to run. You might be able to whip him into running if you hook him up with three or four older dogs and give him a whipping. I've got them to working that way, but they were never really willing workers on my team. They were always drivers. Try petting a couple of times before you go to whipping. A willing dog is a better dog than one you have to push. Any time you are pushing one dog in your team, the rest of the team knows by the tone of your voice that you are pushing somebody, and you want to keep away from that as much as you could.

A dog that drags back and yells and throws himself down, I just wouldn't monkey with. I'd put him away right now. He's already got that crook in his mind that I don't know how you could get rid of. Somewhere along the line he would cause you trouble.

What faults in pups are so bad that you discard them immediately?

One of the main things you want to keep away from is scaring a pup when you hook him up. That first trip has got to be a fun trip. If it isn't, when that pup is a year or a year and a half old, you are going to end up with a dog that is looking back at you all the time because he is scared, or a dog that is scared to run when they are wide open, or with a dog that is scared to run downhill.

I especially wouldn't have anything to do with the dog that looks back because that's pretty easy to pick up. When a dog in your team looks back, and looks back, and keeps looking back, the whole team knows that dog is looking back, and pretty soon the rest of the dogs are looking back. So it's best to discard that one.

If you have a dog that is scared to run fast, the rest of the pups sense that too.

When you are breaking a pup on the first hookup and you get going too fast on a little downhill, the pup can get scared of going downhill and never get over it. That is one of the hardest things to get out of him. When you are working with a bunch of pups and you have one that is scared to run downhill, the rest of the pups sense that too.

Any one of these three dogs — a dog that looks back, or one that is scared when the team runs wide open, or a dog that is scared to run downhill — I wouldn't have anything to do with. I'd get rid of them right now. Of course if you had nothing but time on your hands to work them out of it, I believe you could. But with me, when I start working the team about the 10th of October, I have to be training my grown dogs at the same time as I am working with my pups, so I can't be monkeying around with a dog that is scared of any of these three things.

Another point to watch is the way that back tugline moves when a pup is running. This is after a couple of weeks when the pups know what it is all about. I am looking at that tugline when I am training these pups. Sometimes you find a six and a half to nine months old pup who is running smooth but his back line is not staying steady. He is either slacking off when he is taking off on a jump or he is slacking off when he is coming down on his front quarters. I call this pup a jerk runner. Actually, he is not a bum dog. Usually he has enough speed to stay up with your team. A dog like this could help you if you were short of dogs.

I never have been able to correct that jerk runner to where he did get to run smooth. This kind, even when they grow up to a year or two, are still the same. You might be able to drive him so that he is working so hard that his line is pretty near always tight, but I wouldn't want to have to do that.

I break my pups, and when they are maybe nine months in April, I tie them up for the summer. When I hook them up again in the fall, the dogs that had that jerk run last spring still have it. It would still be right there. I don't care how many ways a dog's legs are flying. If they are flying in all directions, it don't make no difference to me, just so long as when that dog is moving his back line is staying tight. If it isn't, I wouldn't monkey with a pup like that. I'd discard him right now.

BUILD

What do you look for in the build of a dog?

I don't think I could tell anybody how to look at a dog and say, "This is a good one," or "This is a bad one." I couldn't explain it. Like this summer I was clean through Alaska on the Yukon River, and I was in every village looking at dogs. The first village that had a good looking dog was

Tuffy's son Ganja. "This is a wonderfully built dog." Shoulder to hip bone measures 18"; shoulder to ground measures 23½"; weight 56 pounds; color, red.
(photo by Brent Lindstrom)

Grayling. I mean I went through the whole village and I picked this one dog. I figured, "Well, this dog looks like he can run." So I bought this dog and today I got it running in my team and it is going real good.

But I couldn't tell you what was wrong with the rest of the maybe 500 dogs I saw. They were just not what I was looking for.

Maybe the best way around it is to take pictures of some dogs that I think are well built and let whoever looks at the pictures decide what is good about them. Or anybody could go to a big race and take a look at the top five teams. You'd learn more doing it that way than I could teach you by trying to tell you.

What do you look for in a dog's gait?

I look for the dog with the back tugline that don't slack

Little Toughie
"You can't go wrong with dogs built like these two."

Jarvi
"He was in lead every heat of the North American in 69, 70, 71. In 72 he was in swing the first two days, but was in lead for the 30 mile on the last day."

up whether he is taking off on a jump or coming down on his front legs. I talked quite a bit about this back when I was talking about training pups. You know, about the jerk dog.

What is the best weight for a good racing dog?

I like bigger dogs. Right around 50 pounds. I don't think they could go too much faster than the smaller dog, but it is just that you got a lot of power if you want to drive. Say you are getting left behind two minutes in a race. Maybe some of your dogs are tired. But you really want to drive. With a 50 pound dog that is not tired, when you start driving him you are really going somewhere.

I've seen some 60 pound dogs that made good racing dogs, but they are very few. They have to be really outstanding in order to carry that much weight in a 30 mile race and still be winning it.

The smallest I would go for is say 35 pounds. I'd say smaller dogs could probably outdistance the bigger dogs. They could probably stay with it a lot longer than the bigger dogs can.

Actually, in my team probably the smallest dog I've got is pretty close to 40 pounds, and the biggest dog is probably right around 55 pounds.

How do you know how much the dogs weigh?

It's usually just by looking at them. By looking at a dog's size you could tell if he is over 60 pounds or not. You could tell if a dog is too big for running. And then if he's so small he don't look like he could pull that much, then you don't use him either.

Is there anything about the way a dog acts in the lot that tells you if he would make a good race dog?

You get happy ones, and you get the ones that are scared of you. There's no way you can tell by their actions.

Do you think heart can make up for a bad build?

No, I don't think so. A dog with a bad build has got to break down somewhere. There's no way heart can make up for a dog that keeps breaking down.

If a person can keep only a few dogs and plans to enter only the five to seven dog class, would you suggest that he go for

a larger size dog than is common on big teams?

Yes. Like I say, I go for the bigger dog anyhow. I go for the 50 pound dog more than the 35 pound dog because you got more power. If you are going to run only five to seven dogs, you are not going to run very long races anyhow. At least, now, I wouldn't.

FEEDING AND WATERING

Is it true that Indians and Eskimos feed their dogs only every other day in the summer?

I believe this could be true in some cases. But ever since I was a kid, the dogs I have been around ate every day.

What do people in the villages usually feed their dogs?

Fish and rice. We catch dog salmon in the summer that run a little bigger than six pounds. We dry them and store them for the winter. The dogs get roughly one fish a day. And they get meat in the winter, too. That's what I always fed until Penney's started to sponsor me.

Let me tell you about this one. In 1962 I brought my team into Anchorage to race. I ran out of fish before the State Championship at Kenai. So I bought some commercial food and gave it to the dogs, and the dogs got sick. Well, I worried and worried and finally got a veterinarian to come out and look at the dogs. He said it was just the change of food and they would get over it all right. I raced most of the dogs, sick or not, but I left my leader Tuffy out. Leaving him out lost the race for me. I will never forget it.

What do you feed as a summer maintenance diet?

Well, right now Penney's is my sponsor and they are paying the bills, so I am feeding Kasco all summer.

Do you change the dogs' diet as training begins?

Yes. I still feed Kasco, but then I start adding liver to the Kasco. I feed canned liver or a good grade of raw, ground liver. Sometimes I add canned dog meat. For 21 dogs I'll add six cans of liver and three of meat. And I add wheat germ oil when I can get it. That stuff can be hard to find.

How much weight do you like your dogs to carry in summer as compared to when they are in training?

I like to have my dogs a little bit overweight in the summertime and in the fall before I start working them. I found in past years that a dog is really not hard to keep all through the winter if he is a little bit overweight to start with.

If you start him underweight, that dog is going to take a lot of feeding just to bring him up to where he is supposed to be. I have never had one get fat during the winter that was skinny when I started training. So actually, I like to have mine a little overweight and then bring them down as I start training them.

Do you feed at the same hour every day, even if you are away from home?

I believe it upsets their stomach if you zigzag their feeding around too much. It gets dark right now about four o'clock, so I feed about four. I would really like to feed right around five o'clock every night. But a lot of times I'm pressed for time, so sometimes I feed a little later than that when I'm training.

How much weight do you like your dogs to carry just before a race?

Two weeks before a race you should watch it that your dogs are not too fat and not too skinny. Sometimes I find a

"....right around five o'clock every night."

couple of weeks before a race that my dogs are a little underweight. Then in the morning I start feeding them about a cup of rice, honey and cottage cheese. If you keep this up, they put on weight in about a week.

If they are too fat, it is hard to cut their feed down. It is safer two weeks before the race to start putting more weight on, if the dogs need it, than to cut that team's feed down. If you have to cut weight down two weeks before a race, the only way to do it is to work them a little harder.

But either of those two things you don't want to have to do two weeks before the race, if you want the best performance out of your dogs.

How do you feel about weight for a three day race?

Going into a three day race a dog should be a little bit overweight. You could always plan on a lot of power on the third day if your dogs are just a little bit overweight to start with.

About three weeks before a three day race, I start giving a little rice, cottage cheese, honey and Wesson oil in the morning. If I got a race at one o'clock, I feed this mixture about eight o'clock in the morning. And not really much — about a cup of feed to each dog. When you start this, and your dogs are already up to weight, you are naturally going to have to cut down on their evening feed. I usually feed this diet all the way through the race. Right through the three day race.

What would cause you to change the diet of any of your dogs?

I don't think I would change the diet of any of my dogs except for just one reason — no money.

How do you determine if your dogs are too fat or too thin?

Usually by the feel of their ribs is how I go. I never weigh my dogs or anything like that. I just pet them to feel their ribs and see how much meat they've got on them. What I am looking for is just a little layer of fat between the skin and their ribs. The smaller dogs ought to have a little more fat than the big ones. And when it gets cold, they all got to be fatter.

How much weight a dog should carry is kind of up to each

dog itself. Some of the dogs run better when they look like they are overweight, and some of them have to be pretty thin. In past years I would have some of my dogs pretty skinny, and they would get hurt over the winter. Then the next year I would try more weight on them and that would seem better. It all depends on the dog itself.

When your dogs live on snow in the winter, do you water them? If so, how often do you water?

Yeh, I always water my dogs. When I'm just training, I water them twice a day, once in the morning and once in the evening. During the races sometimes I give them about a cup of water two hours before the race.

Roughly I would say I let them have four cups in the morning and four cups in the evening. A lot of my dogs look like beer drinkers. They got pot bellies. I could be wrong, but I really believe a dog needs that much water. So that is the way I do it.

Do you put anything in the water to encourage your dogs to drink more?

Yeh, I always do that. They still grab snow, you know, but not near as much. I use leftovers from the table or just anything to flavor the water. When I'm traveling I use canned dog meat. I'll use one can of beef chunks to four gallons of water.

One time a dog tried to grab snow when the team was moving real fast. It was just a little narrow track, and he fell off the trail. He was dragging before he knew it. Just that fast. So it's important to make them drink water.

I give them warm water in the winter. When I'm at a place where there isn't any hot water, what I do is I have a few buckets of water sitting around the house all the time warming up. If I can, I put buckets on top of the stove. As soon as I empty one bucket, I fill it up again so it can get warm.

If you got to chop a hole in the ice to get your water — like maybe the pump in the house works too slow — then I fill that hole up with snow. The snow keeps the water hole from freezing over, even in 50 below. I like to do everything the easy way if I can.

Racing Breakfast

Do you have any special exercise routine or any special diet for yourself to get yourself in shape for racing?

No, I never do nothing like that.

CHANGING OWNERS

Do you think it is advisable for a person to try out a dog before buying?

No. I don't believe in trying a dog out. I don't believe in giving a dog a trial run. I don't think it is fair to the dog. I don't think a person could take anybody else's dog and just expect that dog to start working for you like your own dog would. I've bought dogs that I've kept around for a month before they actually started doing something for me.

About the only thing you could see with a trial run is if he has a smooth gait or not. By a smooth gait I mean is that line tight 100 percent of the time. Well, maybe not quite 100 percent, but when he hits the ground or is off the ground, that line should always be tight. There is no jerking whatsoever. That is what I would be looking for. With just one run you could spot that.

Mostly it all depends on where you are buying from. Let's say you were number 10 in a race, and you wanted to buy from someone who finished two positions up from you. Buying from somebody that has beaten you, there isn't any reason to try the dog out because if the dog couldn't fit in your team, how did he beat you in the first place? He naturally has to be as good or better than what you've got.

If the dog is a young dog and from a good line of breeding, then there is no need to try him out either.

Buying dogs is actually a big gamble. It's like raising pups. You don't know whether you are going to get a top dog or just what you're really going to get. If you have seen the dog perform and if he is winning races, sure, great, then you are bound to be getting a good dog. But if you are buying a dog that is in say 15th place, then actually you are gambling.

From the seller's point of view, how do you feel about lending a dog out for a trial period?

If I could get around it, I wouldn't lend any of my dogs out for a trial period. Actually, you are trying to sell that dog. Either he has proven that he could win the race, or he is out of a good strain of dogs, or I say that he is good. Well, maybe he wouldn't work for the person you loaned him to, or the person wasn't satisfied because he wasn't the kind of dog he was looking for. So you got the dog back. Well, everybody in town knows that dog and that the person wasn't satisfied. Actually, you have ruined that dog's reputation just by lending him out and not being able to sell him. Then you have to do it all over again. You have to race with the dog and prove how good he is before you can sell him. So for me, I just don't believe in lending dogs out for a trial.

Do you ever sell dogs that can't make it in your team?

When I start training dogs in the fall, anything that can't keep up with the rest goes to the happy hunting grounds. Maybe the ones that are left aren't all the best dogs in the world, but they are doing their part in the team.

Well, pretty soon the training gets tougher, and I got to cut down on the number of dogs I am going to keep. So some of them got to go. I saw one dog here a couple of days ago. That dog couldn't make it for me when I got up to 20 miles, so I sold him to another guy. With that team he slowed down a couple of minutes. He is running the 20 miles now and coming in the money. But with my team running a couple of minutes faster, the dog couldn't make it. He was just a notch below what I wanted. He was just two minutes too slow.

How do you go about buying a new dog?

I just go by what the person tells me. I go by the reputation of the dog and the reputation of the musher that's telling me he has a good dog for sale. And I go by my own reputation.

Most of the dogs I have bought are from right around here locally, from Allakaket and Hughes and Tanana. I got a few from Koyukuk and this area. I go into a yard one time.

All the guys know me. They know that if they sell me a bum dog — that is, a dog that is really no good — then I won't go back to their yard to buy another dog. If I get one out of three, well, I think that is a pretty good buy. But if I get three bums, then I don't go back in that yard again, even if I hear that guy has got three more really outstanding dogs.

I bought a dog here last year from one of the local drivers. This was in Fairbanks in 1970. Warner Vent came in from Huslia for the race as a spectator. He wanted to sell me this one dog. This dog's name was Tootsie. He wanted quite a bit for it, and I was really hesitating about buying it. But he kept insisting that this was a good dog. He had a litter of four pups and he wasn't actually running them on a sled. He was running them with a snow traveler. They were chasing him all over, every place he went. He said he couldn't leave this one dog behind. He told me, "I'll bet my reputation as a dog driver that this dog is a top notch dog and will make any team. I am betting all I know about dogs saying this dog is good, and I am either a dog driver or not a dog driver."

Well, when he talked to me that way, and by knowing Warner Vent and his dog driving, if the guy wants to put it that way he is laying quite a bit on the line. So I went ahead and bought the dog. And by God, the dog is a top notch dog!

If a dog worked well for his owner but not for a new driver, how long should the new driver work on him before giving up?

Well, that is a little hard to say. It all depends. Let's say the dog has been beating you. Okay, he must be as good as anything you got because the guy couldn't have been beating you if he had been dragging that dog on the neckline for any length of time. He wouldn't have been beating you unless you were dragging a bunch of dogs too. So it is up to you, as a dog man, to get the best there is out of that dog.

Sometimes it takes a long time for a dog to get used to a new owner, especially a dog that has been attached to its owner before. Sometimes it takes a couple of months before that dog comes around and starts working for you. I've had dogs for two months before getting anything out of them. I'd never whip any dog until I had run it just easy for at least two months.

To be honest with you, all the good leaders that I have had I didn't raise. Let's take three of the best, as far as command leaders go. Okay, there's Nellie, Tuffy and Blue. Those three dogs I didn't raise. When I got them they wouldn't work for me.

Nellie was three, three and a half when I got her. Nobody ever raced her because they couldn't get no work out of her. I could see that the dog had it so I kept working on it and working on it. I just ran her day after day without saying nothing. I remember I drove Nellie, oh, it must have been a month and a half before she started performing for me.

Tuffy was the same way. He wouldn't work for nobody but the owner, who was Sidney Huntington at the time. He was roughly three and a half years old when I got him. When I got Tuffy, I could see the dog had it. He was smart and he knew his commands perfectly. But then he wouldn't work for me. So I kept working with him and working with him, just running him easy. Then when he did give it to me, he started giving me everything that I knew he had.

Blue was the same way. She was probably the worst one of them all. When I got her she was four years old and nobody had been racing her. I could see this dog had it, but she just wouldn't put out for me. And this is a friendly dog. She jumps on me every time I go out there in the yard. So I just kept working with her and working with her, and by the end of the second month she started working. Blue was never the fastest dog in the world, but for honesty you couldn't ask for a better dog. She will just not go wrong on you.

The main thing, when you see a dog that has got it, and he is not giving you the best he has got, you don't want to lose your patience with the dog. You want to let him come on it by himself. You don't want to have to beat him into it. And some of them take a long time to accept you. These three dogs were sort of unusual in getting used to me.

I've had other command leaders that I would say were about the same quality. There was Johnny. Merv Hilpipre in Iowa has Johnny now. And there was Buster who is living with Ann Wing in New York. I got these dogs after they were trained into command leaders. But these two dogs were completely different. They took to me right away, and they started working the first time I hooked them up.

Tuffy was not an overly friendly dog. He never did want to be bothered. And Nellie was not really all that friendly. But then Blue, Johnny and Buster were all friendly dogs. So you can't really say the reason they didn't work for me was because they were unfriendly. Really hard to say what type dog will work for you right off the bat and what type won't.

Team dogs are the same as leaders. Sometimes they will take to you right away and sometimes they won't. The biggest percent of race dogs will take to working right away because all they know is just working. But some take longer than others. I've carried dogs a year that I knew had it but wouldn't give it to me. I carried them over, and the next year they gave it to me.

It is up to the musher to spot the dog that has got it. Like I say, they got that smooth run. From there it is up to you. They got this for you, and it is up to you to do the rest.

EQUIPMENT--
Sleds, Lines, Harnesses, Accessories

What is your brake like?

It is a piece of wood with a metal claw on the end. It always worked real good until this year. This year I broke my brake just out of the chute the first day of the Ely race, and then I broke another brake the last day of Rendezvous. I ran scared at Ely. At Rendezvous I was lucky the dogs didn't get into any trouble. Maybe next year I will do something about that brake.

Do you use any special kind of brake on your trapline sled?

I just have the regular brake. But when the sled has a heavy load and you have to go down a steep hill, you can slow the sled down by wrapping rope or a chain a few times around the runners. Put it on at the top and take it off at the bottom.

Do you use a different sled for training than you do for racing?

No, I use my racing sleds on training runs.

What is the length of your runners?

You are going to stand on the runners at the back of the stanchion. Maybe you got 3 or 3½ feet of runner in front of you. Your feet should be riding right in the middle of the runner where you figure it's going to touch the snow. Or maybe it could be a couple of inches longer in back of your feet. It all depends on how you ride. If the sled doesn't corner right, if it rides too straight on turns and doesn't make them smooth, then your runners are too long in the back.

Would you tell us about the surface of your sled runners?

P-Tex — that ski runner plastic — and steel runners are about all I run on. It's band-saw steel. I've used wax on P-Tex, but I really don't know that much about wax to experiment. Maybe you put the wrong kind of wax on and the sled would pull hard. With just steel on one sled and P-Tex on another sled you could pretty much pick your weather. If it is thawing, you stick to your metal and you have an easy running sled. If it is below freezing, P-Tex goes pretty good.

A racer recently said that he lost because his runners were the wrong width for the snow and condition of the trail. Do you think different width runners should be used?

I have pretty much standardized mine. They are an inch and three quarters, and the spacing between the stanchions is 18″. I use the same width all the time.

About the racer saying he lost because his runners were the wrong width, I don't think there is any such thing. If he had a good enough dog team I don't think he would have to blame it on his runners.

What is the length of your basket?

They are roughly between 3½ and 4 feet.

How much do the sleds you build weigh?

The sleds I build weigh, oh, I would say right around 20 pounds.

What kind of wood do you prefer in sleds?

I really prefer birch, but the last few years I have been using a lot of white ash just for the reason that it is already cut. I prefer birch to any hardwood because it's got more flexibility to it. You could push it in more ways than any other wood that I have worked with.

In fact, where I am making this tape right now is in my shop. This is the only place I can get some quiet around here. I go down to the house and I got six wild Indians in

Sleds and dog truck, 1970 Rendezvous. Handler, Karen Manook (now Karen Attla). (photo by Maxine Vehlow)

there raising hell, and you can't very well get anything done on a tape down there.

Is weight or flexibility more important in a sled?

I don't think seven or eight pounds in a sled makes that much difference. It is the way the sled rides, how limber it is.

I try to make my sleds as flexible as I can. But a sled doesn't really get the limber on it until after you use it for a while. When it's first made then it's a little stiff, but after a couple of runs, then it limbers up. Like with my sled, I could take that thing and completely twist it around turns to where I would never — well, I can't say never because I have done it — but there would be very few times that I would end up upside down.

I've tried those sleds that had hinges on the stanchions. You could twist them and ride them around the turn. But I'd rather stick with mine.

These stiffer sleds that have been brought up from back East, I've tried them out quite a bit. Maybe on straight going those sleds are probably just as good as what I got, but when it comes to cornering for me, they just don't corner as good.

It may be in the wood too. This birch I use is not really hard wood. You could twist it any way if you get the right kind of birch with a straight grain. What I do is I go out in the woods and I don't just chop down any birch. I go through a whole bunch of birch testing for grain until I find the kind of birch I want with the grain running the right way. Then that is what I use. You could twist this wood any way you want. That is the reason for the limber sled, I think.

No more about sleds. I wouldn't want to try to tell somebody how to build a sled. I don't mean that mine are the best, but they are the best for me. I tried sleds that are built by other people, but I could never handle them as well as I could mine.

Do you prefer a snap on the neckline or a loop that goes over the dog's head?

I really prefer the loop over the snap. Maybe it is because I have been using the loop such a long time. But this winter I had a lot of experience I never had before. I had to do

Harness and lines, 1970 Rendezvous. (photo by Maxine Vehlow)

more changing dogs around in the middle of a race than I ever had to do in my whole life. I found experimenting with the snaps and the loop that I could do the snap faster than I could do the loop. So I think that after this for races I will take to the snap and leave the loop out.

I like the loop for my training runs when it is colder. I just slip it behind the collar and over his head and I got my dog hooked up. A lot of times when it is cold the snaps freeze. You could eliminate all the trouble with freezing in your training runs by using the loop. The dogs will not be upset by the difference because they both work off the neck.

Do trapline teams have a different type harness than the race teams?

No, not really they don't. They used to have work harnesses, you know, the collar harness. But right now the guys that are still using dogs for trapline work just use the same type of harness that I use.

Do you have a different design harness for training than for racing?

No. I use the same harness that I race with.

What design harness do you favor for racing?

Well, I like the Fishback harness better than any other racing harness. They are well put together. Actually, those Fishback harnesses are the very same type harness that we've been using around here for years.

Do you have a special harness for each dog?

No. I just use small, medium and large.

How do you like your harnesses to fit?

Usually you can tell if a harness don't fit a dog by the way it rides on him when he's not pulling. It should be smooth all over him. If it's humped on his back, the harness is too small. Sometimes a small dog will have a big chest and it will take a large harness to fit him right.

I like my snaps to come right about even with the hip bone.

Some harnesses I've seen have no business being on the market. There ought to be a law against them. I've seen them at stores. They just weren't built for dogs to work in. They were wrong around the throat. If a dog tried to work in one of them, it would have choked him.

At the North American one year it was the other way. I was watching the teams go out in the freight race. The harness on this one dog was so big that he kept going through it, and the handlers were there pulling that collar back. I never met the musher before, but that dog must have gone around the track with his legs tied up with that big harness.

That was terrible!
How do you make your lines?

I make my lines out of braided polyethylene rope. The measurements got to be right. You want the dogs to be able to be free to run without getting choked, but you don't want everything so loose that they get messed up, like being able to put a front foot over the neckline.

Talking about being able to run free, remember when I was telling you about that race I ran as a kid when I used my father's dogs? You know I was in the hospital all during this time, and when I came back I was big enough to get in the seniors. But I lost most of what I learned. When I started to get into it, my dad had good dogs. I guess maybe some of the guys were worried about me, that I might beat them, and they started telling me about these short lines they use in Fairbanks. Foot long backlines. And I didn't even have my own lines — everything there belonged to my dad. Anyway, I went to work on the towlines the night before the race. I started cutting the towlines up, and I made all the backlines a foot long. I didn't know any better. That was really stupid. The next day when the dogs stepped off, they couldn't run. They were too close together. They were afraid of jumping on each other. Everybody was jumping straight up in the air, not covering any ground. It really taught me something.

Anyhow, I'll get on with the measurements here.

The wheelers' tugs are 55". The team dogs' tugs are 40". The leaders' tugs are 30". I make all my measurements to the end of the snap.

The necklines are all 14" for each dog, except the leaders' double neckline is 14".

From where the line is attached to the sled to where the wheelers' tuglines are attached is 6". From the wheel dogs' necklines to where the next pair of tuglines is attached is 20". From the swing dogs' necklines to the leaders' tugs is 30". That last measurement can be changed to 40" to the leaders' tugs, but then you shorten the tugs to 20".

I allow 33" in the gangline for each dog's harness. The

FISHBACK HARNESS

DOUBLE NECKLINE

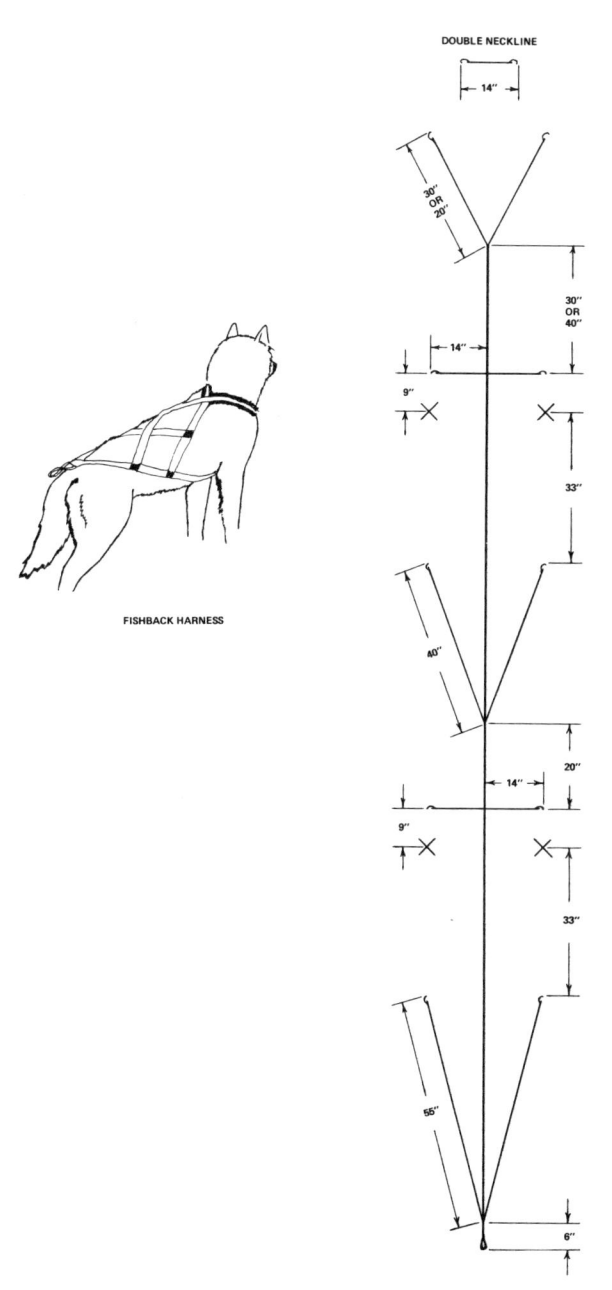

|← 14" →|

30" OR 20"

30" OR 40"

|← 14" →|

9"

33"

40"

|← 14" →|

20"

9"

33"

55"

6"

GEORGE'S TOWLINE

way I get that is I measure from where the harness attaches at the snap to the cross at the back of the neck. I use Fishback harnesses so the measurement is to where those harnesses cross. I adjust the loop at the back of the harness to get the 33".

The most important measurement in the whole line is: when the harness is snapped to the tug and stretched out, *the distance between the cross at the back of the neck and the neckline must be 9"*.

To get the distance in the gangline between where the tug attaches and where the neckline attaches, just add the length of the tugline, the 33" for the harness and 9".

I use the same lengths for every harness and every dog and every line. Every hookup is the same.

What is your snow hook like?

I have a special design snow hook that I had made up. It is shaped so that the more the dogs pull, the deeper it goes into the snow. It is one hook. I push it in the ground and then call the dogs to go forward to set it. Depending on the trail, it works pretty good.

If there is a tree near where I stop, I throw the hook around the tree. That can be safer.

Let me tell you what happened one time. On the third day of the Fairbanks race they add on a 10 mile loop to the 20 mile course. The first two days of the race this loop is blocked off with snow fence. Well, this third day I was going out first, and when I got to where the trail turned off for the new 10 mile loop, nobody had been out to take the snow fence down. I knew I had to go down that loop so I stopped the team. A fellow was standing there with a camera, and I yelled to him to take the snow fence away. But the darn guy just stood there taking pictures. I was cussing him out as I set the snow hook and went to take the fence down. I got even madder when some guy's team started to pass me up just as I was getting the fence down. Well, this team was just about by me when I realized it was my own team. I almost missed the sled as it went by, but I did manage to get it. The team had pulled the hook. Thank God the leaders had

Weight 6 pounds

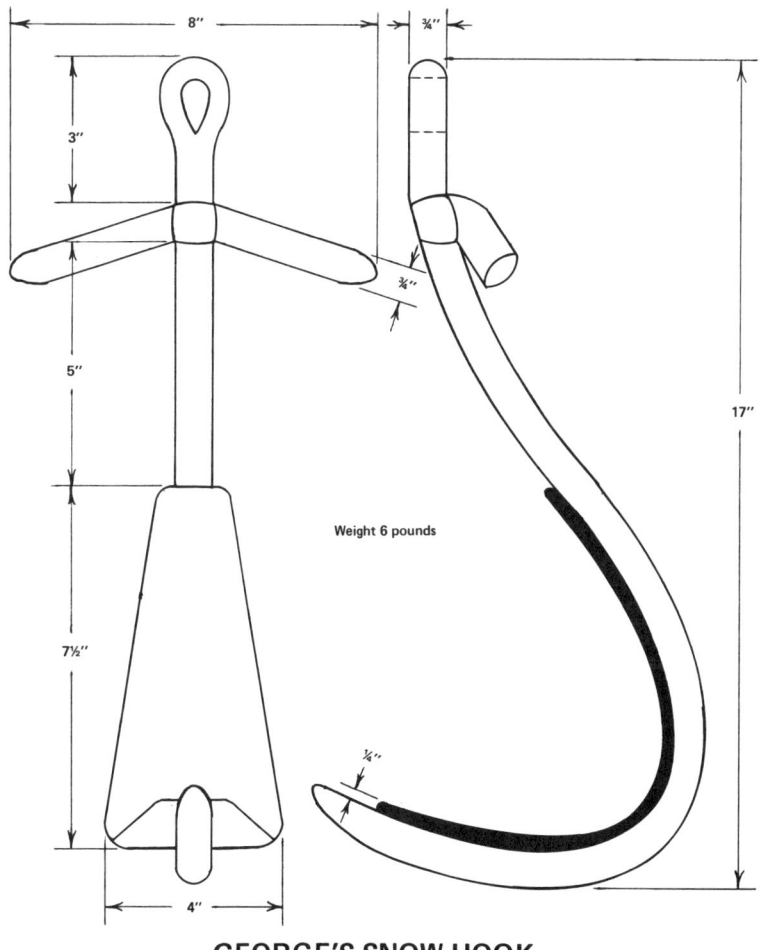

GEORGE'S SNOW HOOK

99

decided to go down the new loop. If they had gone down the trail they had run for two days, I would have had it! (He won that race anyhow. Ed.)

Do you use shock cord in your lines?

No. I use it under the sled in the bridle. That way it takes the jolts off the whole team.

How do you keep a dog in the basket?

I usually have a line on each of my front stanchions and a line on each of my back stanchions. I snap the line on the front stanchion to the back end of the dog, and I snap the line on the back stanchion to the dog's neck. That way I have a pretty good hookup on him.

I notice some people use bags and they zip their dogs up in them. Probably this is a better method, but I just never got around to making one.

What do you use for jinglers?

Usually they are just beer bottle caps.

What gear is carried in the sled bag for a long race?

I carry — let me tell you about what happened here a little while ago. I ran through, oh, about a page of these questions and I was ready to listen to myself. I tried it out and the doggone thing didn't record. So actually I am answering the same questions I answered a little while ago.

This is what I carry. I carry my jinglers in my pocket and the whip I have in the bag. The whip and the jinglers are with me all the time. And the dogs know that they are with me all the time.

And I carry, oh, about a 6' length of 1/4" line, just in case something breaks and I need it. And I make about 3" loops out of 1/8" polyethylene. I usually carry a bunch of those in case something gives. Another thing, I always carry an extra pair of gloves when I am racing.

And oranges. I always carry oranges when I am racing. I got two oranges that are sliced up in my bag at the start of a race. Maybe I don't use the whole thing, but that is what I start out with. When I am working hard, really getting everything out of myself, I always seem to dry up. What I do with those is I just wet my mouth with them. Maybe an

"I always carry oranges when I am racing." 1970 Rendezvous.

(photo by Maxine Vehlow)

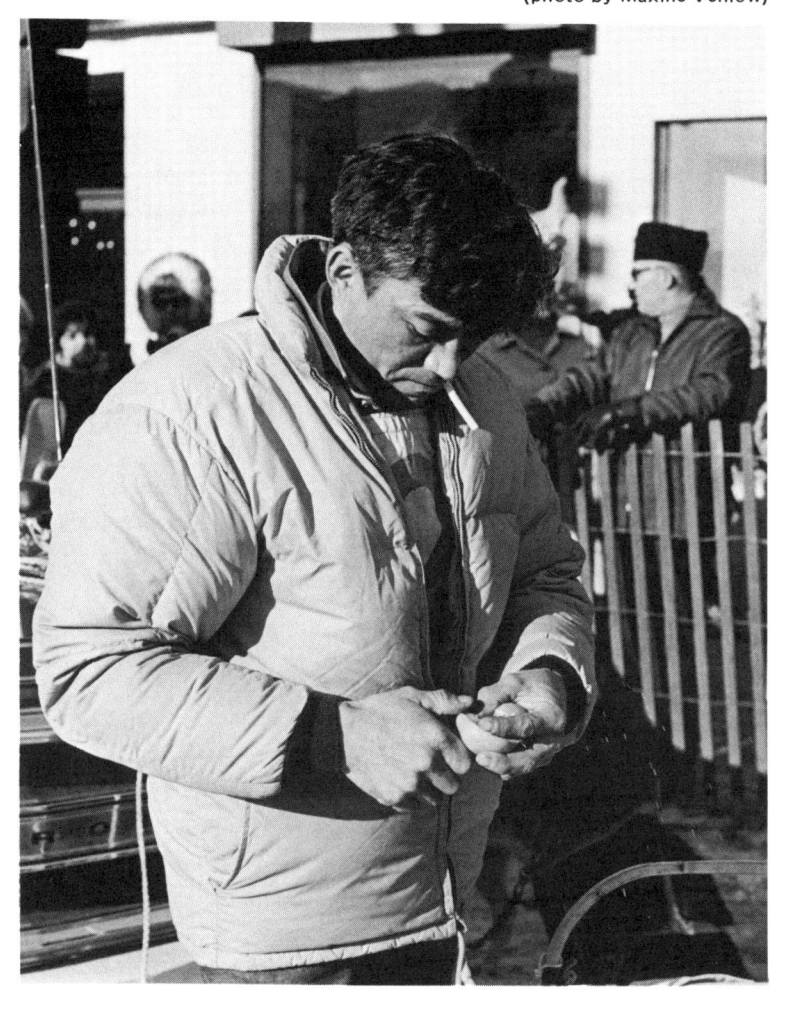

orange wouldn't be the best thing for you, but you just need something to put moisture in your mouth.

Is anything special carried on your person?

Yeh, a pocket knife. The reason I carry a pocket knife is not that I think I am going to get in a big mess and the only way I am going to get out is to cut my way out of it. The only thing I am thinking about when I put that knife in my pocket at the start of a race is that I may have misjudged one of the dogs. This is always a possibility. So the fastest way I am going to get that dog out of his position is just to cut him out of there, cut his neckline and his backline. Instead of unhooking him and then hooking his lines on to the other dogs, I'll just cut him out. So that is the idea of the pocket knife.

If you got into a big enough mess that you were hurting some dogs and the only way out of it is by cutting lines, then that knife would come in handy too. But for me, that don't enter my mind.

Another thing I am doing is chewing gum all the time. When I get done with the race, and get home and let all my dogs out and sit down to relax with a cup of coffee, and throw my gum away, I rub my jaws and find they are just as tired as my legs. It must be nerves.

DOG PSYCHOLOGY

How much affection do your dogs get in the dog lot?

First thing when I go out in the morning, I go water my dogs. I like to make it a fun thing for them. If you had that much time you could pet them. There is no harm in petting them, but I just talk to the whole bunch happily. You know, sort of waken the whole team up. Make them feel good.

Then during the day when I am going to take them in the truck, I make that fun for them too. In fact, I pet every dog I throw in. I do the same thing when I take them out. I pet them as I snap them on their chains. I like to see a dog team lively, so hooking them up I try to make it fun for them. When you are in heavy training it is hard to keep their attitude up. At feeding time maybe I don't pet them, but I talk to them.

During the day if I go out there and pet one dog, I go through the whole team and pet them all. I don't believe in petting just one dog. If a bunch of people is around and I go over to one dog, if he is a friendly dog he naturally jumps on me. So you know me, I can't keep my hands off the dog so I go ahead and pet him anyway. But there is a lot of people around so the other dogs' attention is not all focused on me.

I want to be friends with all my dogs. When I go out in the dog lot, I like to see them jump on me, and stuff like that. I don't discourage them. If they want to jump on me, they jump on me.

Some drivers say that they do not like to use dogs again that have been carried in the basket. They believe that the dog has learned a bad lesson. Would you use a dog again that had been carried in a race?

I believe that when a dog just flat lays down and quits on you, he is never going to get over that. By quitting I mean that he didn't pass out from being exhausted. He just quit because he figured, "Well, I've had enough of this."

Even next year, when you are in a hard race, when you are behind by just a little bit, this dog may do the same thing he did last year. In a race you are not on a training run. When he quits the only thing you could do is just load him in the basket and haul him home. So once you load a dog in the basket he has always got it in his head that I got away with it last time and I didn't get nothing for it. As far as I know, there is no way you could take this lesson back out of his mind.

But I've carried a dog in a race and then ran him again the next year in the same race, and he has made it for me. The only reason I did it though was because I knew he had a good reason for going down. I've had dogs go lame, maybe on the last run before a race. I've put in a dog that I knew was lame. I didn't admit it then, but I admitted it after the dog went down. I started thinking, "How did he run that last time?" What it boils down to is that I wanted to run that dog so bad I didn't want to admit he was hurting when I put him in.

How does it work to borrow a dog and put him in your team right before a race?

One thing I have learned from past experience is that you can't pick up a dog two weeks before a race and expect to win with that dog. I don't care how good he is, he is not going to respond to you like the dogs you have been working with all winter.

I have done this in the past, like when I borrowed those five dogs from Bill Williams in 1962. But that is the only time it ever worked for me. I did it last winter too. Last winter I was running short of dogs so I went and rented four dogs from Carl Huntington. They were good dogs, just as good as anything I had, but I only had them for two weeks before the North American. Actually what happened was this one dog, Tex, was a leader, and I put her in lead to start out with the first day. The dog was a top notch dog, but she wasn't used to a high powered team putting pressure on her like mine did. Those dogs started out really moving, and at ten miles out she started acting up. At twelve miles she just pulled the whole team over to the side and stopped. That's what a new dog will do. No matter how good this dog was, and I really don't believe they come any better, she just wasn't used to that kind of pressure.

So it doesn't pay to get a new dog less than two months before the race, if you plan on winning. I have always preached never do it, never do it, never do it. And I did it. But then sometimes you run short of dogs and there is no way you can get around it.

Why will a dog work better for one musher than another, assuming he knows them both equally well?

Well, the dog may know both the mushers equally well, but the truth is that they don't know the dog equally well. The one that understands that dog best, is the better dog man, and is naturally the one who is going to get more out of the dog.

How do you handle a spook or shy dog?

I try to handle them just as much as I can. If I don't have that much time to spend with this one particular dog, then I try to get somebody else to handle him. Once they are spooky like that, really shy, they don't seem to get over it. But you could cut that down a certain percent when you handle the dog a lot.

Do you feel that you know all of your dogs well and that they all know you? How important is this?

Yes, I do feel that they all know me and that I know all of them well. Actually, I think this is one of the most important things about a dog team. I try to know everything about every dog — how each dog will react to every situation, how much I can get out of them and how much they can give me. They may not be the best, but all I am shooting for is the best that they've got.

How do you treat your dogs when you come in from a run?

I think that the best thing you could do when you come in is to pet the dogs. If there was any training to be done, it should have been done out there on the trail.

How do you get your dogs to respect you but still not be afraid of you?

Well, this is a tough question. First off you have to be sure this dog knows what he is supposed to do. When you give a command to go faster and he doesn't pick it up with the rest of the dogs, he has to have picked up what that command means from the other dogs and responded to it enough times so that you are sure he knows what it means. Maybe his name is Ring. You holler, "Get up, Ring!" You try that three or four times and he doesn't pick it up. Then you go out there with your whip and whip him. Okay, so he picks it up because he knows he was supposed to have been working. After you bring him off the trail, you want to make sure you pet this dog as you are unhooking him, just to show him that you are still friends with him.

When you whip this dog out there, that is putting fear

"Maybe the last couple of miles of a long race...my tone of voice is nothing but fear." Rendezvous 1972, Grover and Jarvi in lead.

(photo by Henry Peck - Anchorage Daily News)

into him. When you bring him in and make friends with him, then he will respect you. I don't know how to relate these two, but he will respect you instead of fearing you. He respects you as his master as opposite to being afraid of you. They work those two out somehow in their minds.

Do you think dogs run best out of fear or because they want to, or somewhere in between?

You can't run just on fear. You can drive your dog team, but you have to be able to play with them too.

Once you have your dog team trained, you have to know by the way they act how much you can drive them. When I holler "Get up!" like I was mad at them, then I am after fear. But dogs can't take running under a steady pressure of fear. When your dogs are already going at their best and you keep yelling for more, which they haven't got, you are going to be in trouble because those dogs' minds are going to give. They are going to look for ways out of it. They are maybe going to take you off the trail or even lay down on you. When the dogs are tired it is very easy for them to break down, unless you have a hard-headed team. So don't keep asking for it and asking for it. Now just fear alone could win on a hard-packed trail that don't take no response. But I wouldn't want to have anything to do with that.

Okay. In between running them out of fear they have to run for the fun of it too. You have to make your voice sound like it's fun. Let's take my team for instance. Usually for the first four or five miles of a race they will go all on their own. They are going just because they want to run. Then after that I have to give a command now and then to pick it up. Maybe the last couple of miles of a long race I have to take my whip out and my tone of voice is nothing but fear. But then if I had to, I could back out of that too, if it don't look like the team could take the pressure. Maybe the team is shot. Then you have to quit this kind of fear altogether and go completely on fun, even if they go down to a trot, just to keep them going, just to finish the race.

When you are getting the best out of a dog, then I think that you are playing right at the edge of the thing. You go to the borderline just between breaking and not breaking. If you go too far your dogs will quit on you. You have to be pretty careful. You have to know your dog team.

ATTITUDE IN HARNESS

Do you ever deliberately get your dogs sour at the beginning of the season so that they learn that they have to run, like it or not?

I don't get my dogs sour on purpose at the beginning of the season. In the fall I start training with short runs. I keep stepping up the miles as I know they could take it. What I try to do is teach them to run because they like it, not because of force.

When you are training steady and your dogs go sour, do you keep pushing them or do you lay off for a while?

When I am in heavy training and they are getting kind of sour, then I slack off and lay them up for a while and try to get a little life back into them. If you go too far when you are training, if you keep pushing past that point, then when your racing time comes all you're racing on is just pure training.

There are times when you need more training miles, you need to keep going. But it is best not to. Try to allow more time to train for a race. You couldn't make a winning team in one month. If you take three months to do it, you've got quite a bit of time to train your team then.

Do you hook up your leader first or last?

What I do when I hook up in a race or in a training run is I hook the dogs first that are not barking or anything, the dogs that are quiet and won't cause trouble. Like maybe all they do is wait for you to hook up the rest of the dogs. I go from there until I hook up the liveliest dog in the whole bunch.

I try to keep out of trouble when I am hooking up in the dog yard. I prefer to hook up my leaders last. The team seems to get a lift when you hook up your leaders last, particularly if it is a female leader. It all depends on what kind of a leader this is too. I got four teams to run in one day with double leads so I am using eight leaders for that day. Not all of them are the best leaders in the world. Maybe not even one of them. They are either goofing up the team or doing something wrong. They know they are doing something wrong, but I don't want to have to touch those dogs when they are right in their dog lot. I never whip a dog in the dog lot unless there is a fight.

If I have one or two dogs, maybe not leaders, that really go wild in harness, then I save these dogs to last. They lift up the spirit of the team on a training run even if your team has gone sour. And in a race they liven your team up. This works both places.

Do you think a dog should be disciplined for jumping and barking when he is being harnessed and hooked up?

No. I think a dog should be as happy as you could keep it before you put it to work. If it is jumping and barking, that is much better.

Your dogs could get to where they are too eager, just tearing up everything so bad you have to have a handler for each dog. I really believe that when they get this lively they are burning up a lot of energy before you even start. It is good to have them barking and jumping, all right, but you don't want to have them tearing the place up either. Usually a well trained dog wouldn't do this anyway.

When you have had your best runs, how was your team acting?

I have always had pretty quiet teams. Maybe a couple of dogs in there were jumping and barking. Actually, I would prefer a jumping, barking team, but after the training they go through, they hardly ever get that jumping and barking back into them. You get some, but they are not as lively as they were like say in October when I first started training them.

What do you do about a dog that works too hard in comparison with the rest of the team?

I've had dogs like this that were really outstanding and worked too hard. Just couldn't slow them down. If you put one like this further up front, maybe he won't work quite so hard.

I'll tell you about this one dog I got now, Scotty. He's been running in my team for, oh, this is his third year now. He's one of Blue's pups. I had a litter of five and I got two outstanding dogs out of this litter of pups. This was the last batch of pups that my mother raised. When she was raising these pups she said she wouldn't raise no more pups after this. He's a leader, not a really good command leader, but I've been running him in the lead since he was 14 months old. He works so hard he just doesn't know how to slack up and give himself a breather. So what he does is he just takes the team off the trail and stops. He don't try to drag me all over the place. All I got to do is go out there and put him back on the trail and then he's off again. When I'm coming into the chute at the finish line you could just see this dog when he's in the lead just towing the whole team. But he works too hard. That's the reason for his bolting I think. I don't think any animal could work that hard and keep it up without stopping somewhere. He is quite a dog.

Have you ever done much winning with a team that had no natural willingness but was working on obedience only?

No, I've never really had much winning with a team like that. Like I say, my team is never really lively, but they know what they got to do. It is just kind of natural for them to be running and listening when I tell them to do something. So usually it is most always a willing team.

Say you are going on a twenty mile race. I'll be going on willingness most of the way. I am just kind of playing with them and not really talking rough to them. But towards the end, then it is usually pure training that I am moving on.

How do you feel that a good team in good condition should act at the end of the season?

Well, usually my team is pretty quiet at the end of the season. Actually they are just tired of running. After racing every weekend for say two months, if you are still winning, well, the thing that is winning for you at that time is just the training that went into them dogs.

TEAM MAKE-UP

Hound-type dogs are popular in parts of Canada that are as

cold as Alaska. They win long races. Do you have any special reason for not using these hound crosses?

The only reason I am not using them is because I'm doing okay with what I got, and it is expensive to experiment. As long as I'm winning with what I got I'll stay with them. When I start losing, then maybe I'll try using the hound crosses, if that's what's beating me. But I really believe in Alaskan dogs.

Does the sex of a dog make any difference to you?

No, not really. But I would prefer males over females because the females make some trouble by coming in heat.

Do you think it wise to run bitches in heat in a race?

This all depends on if any really top bitches in your team are in heat because you are naturally going to run all your top bitches. If you have a well trained team, the bitch in heat is not going to bother the dogs that much. If she is well trained, it won't bother her too much.

Would you rely on a whole litter on one racing team?

If they were good, I would say yes. If every one of them is a top dog on your team, then I would use them.

What do you think of putting dogs of different sizes on the same team?

The size of a dog doesn't matter so much. What counts is whether they can make it and do their part.

How do you make up your team? Which dogs do you put where and why? After you have placed your dogs, are you strict about keeping them there?

The way I make up my team is by how good the dogs listen to me, how good they respond to me. The dogs that respond are the ones up front. I hardly ever pair up my dogs. Usually any dog could run with any dog. They pretty much have the same stride or they wouldn't be in the team in the first place. Maybe that's a fault in me, but I've never believed in pairing up this certain dog with that certain dog.

When I make up my team — I'm talking about a racing team now, a full 16 dog team — the dogs that are up front are the dogs that are not going to cause me any trouble and are going to run every step of the way without me having to tell them anything. This don't always work, of course. I make mistakes, too. The swing dogs I know would respond to me no matter what and are the easiest to handle. As I go further back, the dogs get a little harder to handle. The harder they are, the closer they are to me so I can get to them.

I experiment all winter moving dogs around to see if I can get a better performance out of a dog somewhere else. If I have a dog in front that is not listening so good, then he just naturally lost his position to somebody else. By the time I hit my first race, I know just where each dog will run best. You shouldn't have to shuffle any dogs during a race. This should be completely eliminated during your training. But it happens to all of us. It's one of those things you can't get away from.

In a three day race, now, if you watch my team, you'll notice a lot of dogs change around from day to day. Maybe it looks like my swing dog is going to have a bad day. Then for that reason I would drop him back four positions and move one of those dogs up to second. I put the swing dog as close to the sled as I can because I may have to cut him out later on. If one of the leaders was not listening good and I got another one I think will work better up front, I'm going to save time by moving these dogs around too. Then there are some dogs that just plain run different the first day from the second day. In a three day race you have to know how each dog is going to act each day.

I don't think I have ever run a team that was hooked up in the same position every day of a three day race. The dogs are always changed around.

What makes you put a dog in wheel?

The wheel dog is one of the toughest dogs in a race team, a really tough dog. Most of the time they are eager and look like they're going to tear the track up when you hook them up. They start out fast. But usually they're a couple of dogs that will run maybe three or four miles just out of that eagerness and then call it quits and fall in with the rest of the team. These dogs know how to pace themselves. They don't just go out and kill themselves the first 15 miles of a 20 mile race. They only work when I tell them to, and the rest of the time they are usually running free.

My wheel dogs are the kind that are backing me up. They are like reserve power. When the rest of the team is getting tired, then I call on these two dogs and they go to work to take a little weight off those dogs further out that have been working harder for me. At the end of the race, like say the last two miles, these dogs have a lot of strength left. When I start talking to the team and I'm asking for everything, then they're really working with all that reserve power. By the time I've finished the race track, they are as tired as the rest of the team.

Really top notch wheelers are hard to come by. I could remember a couple of pairs that I had that were on the wheel all the time. Ring and Stan were running on the wheel there for a couple of years. Then I had Whitey and Slim that I was running together. I sold Whitey and Slim last summer. Then this winter I ran a couple of new ones. With these two wheelers I had to do a lot of shuffling back and forth. (1971, Ed.)

That's a hard job at wheel. With a big string in front of them and the sled behind throwing them around on every curve, those dogs have to know how to handle themselves. They got to be really tough to stand up. That's how I look at wheel dogs.

LEADERS AND LEADER TRAINING

Can you tell us something about early leader training?

You know it was only about 40 years ago that they learned how to make a leader out of a dog. Before that you were the leader and had to be out in front of the team on snowshoes. Just think of all that time that guys were out walking in front of their dogs. I don't know who smartened up and got the idea of making a leader out of one of the

Edwin Simon and Sammy Sam

Bessie and Chief Henry

dogs. And I don't know how he did it. I was always going to ask Chief Henry about that because he was a young man then and would remember. But every time I go to Huslia I get so busy doing other things I forget to ask him.

I think I told you the story, didn't I, about old Edwin? Edwin and two other guys were partners on a trapline. This must have been 50 years ago, or maybe even longer than that because he's 72 now. Edwin was the youngest, so when the three of them went out with the dogs, Edwin was the leader because they didn't have no leader. He was taking orders from the other two guys all the time. All fall he ran ahead of those dogs, every day. He didn't say how big the team was, but it couldn't have been more than four or five dogs because they say four dogs was a big team then.

At Allakaket around New Year's they were having a potlatch. That's where they all get together and have races like foot races. It's sort of a carnival. So Edwin said they were having this eight mile snowshoe race. Four or five miles out in the woods he was ahead of the pack, except for two guys right behind him. They were his two partners, the two guys he was leader for all fall. He said that when he hit the river and started to come back into town, these two passed him just like he was standing still. He said that was the last time he ran ahead of the dogs for those guys. They lost their leader right there.

Is there such a thing as a natural leader? What is it? How can you determine it?

I believe there are some natural leaders. But the only way you are going to spot it is if the dog is running in lead. I've run a lot of really top notch leaders and I never have seen these leaders show how really good they were until I started running them in lead. Some of these leaders I came by were already trained to commands. But a lot of things that they were picking up was not taught to them.

Like I had this leader once I bought from Edwin Simon. His name was Dixie. I believe this was back in 1959. I would say this dog was a natural leader because he was doing things that I didn't know he knew. I remember one day I had 11 dogs and I was running him single lead. I was trapping beaver that day, and at the same time I was running my trapline I was looking for moose. About seven miles from my cabin I spotted a moose. I had my gear ready. My rifle was strapped to my back and my snowshoes were right in the sled ready to grab. Well, when I spotted this moose I just jumped off the sled with my snowshoes. I didn't tell the dogs nothing. It never entered my mind when I jumped off and let that dog team go, "What is going to happen to my dog team? Where are they going to go?"

Well, I followed that moose around for a couple of hours before I finally did manage to get him. Then I came back to the same spot where I let the dogs go a couple of hours before. When I got there, here is my 11 dogs. They were off the trail all strung out and all just lying down there waiting. It was kind of a surprise to me because I didn't really expect that. Actually, I didn't know what to expect. The last time I saw them, they were running wide open. And here I come back two hours later and they are all strung out along the trail just ready to go.

This dog had me scratching my head, you know. I really didn't know what the heck to expect of him. So the next day when I went out running my trapline, I came to a big lake. I had the same 11 dogs, and I jumped off with my snowshoes. I didn't say nothing, just jumped off and let the team go. I wanted to see what was going to happen when that leader found out I wasn't back there. It was a big lake, and he didn't go too far before he found out. And when he found out, he just turned that team around and brought them back to me.

I asked Edwin about it when I got home that evening. I asked him if he had ever lost this Dixie dog before, and he told me, "No." So this dog just got attached to me and came by that by himself. When I wasn't with them, he wouldn't let the team go. He just wouldn't leave me.

It's really amazing, like I was saying the other day, sometimes you get in the middle of a big lake in a snowstorm and you can't see nothing – no shoreline, no trail, no nothing. If you just let your leader have his own head, he never misses the trail. As long as he has been over that trail, he will hit that portage just right every time, as long as you leave him alone. As long as you don't start thinking, "Well, I know better than he does so I've got to tell him which way to go." You can mess them up by doing that and get them lost.

Back when I used to trap, I had leaders like that all the time – Dixie, Speedy, Rex – they never got lost. They got a sense of direction much better than us, you know. And they never forget. Say you took a dog over a trail this year. Five or six years from now if you take this same dog over this same trail, he'll hit the portage right on.

Some leaders feel for the trail with their feet. They feel for the hard bottom. If they fall off the right side, they cut over to the left. They keep weaving back and forth until they pick up the trail again.

In a race you have got to be thinking for your dogs all the time. You got to know what they can and what they can't do. But when it comes to being out on a trapline in a blizzard, you had better let the dogs think for themselves.

Have you seen any particular signs in any of your leaders while they were still pups that made you think they had lead dog potential?

No, not really. I pick the pup that is the most willing and the one that is working the hardest and try him in lead. If I have a litter of pups that are all hard workers, I try all of them because you really can't tell which one would make a good lead dog.

What is it about a team dog that makes you decide to try him further up or even in lead?

If I got a dog way back in my team that is listening real good to me, then I move him further up. The dog that don't listen, I move him further back. One time or another I try every one of my dogs in lead to see what's going to

"...sometimes you get in the middle of a big lake in a snowstorm and you can't see nothing—no shoreline, no trail, no nothing."

happen.

Another thing that would make me put a dog up in a team would be because he was working harder than he should be. When a dog is working too hard and you put him further in front, he would slack off more.

Do you think that using a team for various publicity stunts such as parades would ruin a lead dog?

I think a good lead dog could be used for just about anything as long as you don't do it too often. I believe you could get away with it without ruining him as long as it is fun for him, as long as you don't demand too much of him.

If you had no other way to go, would you prefer a speed leader or a slower command leader?

If you don't have any choice, it is better for you to keep out of trouble with a dog that is slower and knows his commands and will do what you tell him to do. Even if it takes you a little longer to cover a mile, you would come out ahead in a 20 mile race. With a couple of speed dogs going all over the place you never know where you are going to wind up, but with a good command dog at least you know you are going to be running the trail.

Maybe if you had a race track that the dogs couldn't get off of, no way they could break off the track, then you are better off with those two speed dogs. But if you have a race track with a bunch of road crossings and a lot of people, then actually you are better off with that command dog, even if he is slowing up the team a little.

By a slow command dog I don't mean one that would really hold your team back. I mean one that if you are hitting your top speed maybe this dog couldn't do it. But then you don't hit this top speed very often.

Really it would be best to have two top command dogs. But only once have I been able to come up with two hot dogs at one time, and that was back in 1962 when I came up with both Tuffy and Nellie. They were a once in a lifetime.

How do you feel about hooking up in double lead a speed leader and a slower command leader?

Nellie (the black dog on left) leading the team with Bill William's Judy as Tuffy was sick. Kenai-Soldotna, 1962. Nellie and Tuffy in double lead together won the 1962 Rendezvous for George. *"They were a once in a lifetime."*

(Photograph courtesy of Forrest Shields)

Tuffy, in retirement in California, stands between Daphne Levorsen and Fury on the left, and Knik on the right.

I've done this when I had a command dog that was too slow and I didn't have no other choice. I've had good command dogs that were not as fast as I wanted so I naturally hooked a speed dog up with them. The command dog keeps the team honest. A lot of times on a three day race you have got to change the speed dog around. Maybe you run three different dogs three different days with this command dog.

If this command dog would perform just as good without this speed dog in there, then I would go to a single lead. I've never run single lead, but I would if I had a perfectly dependable command dog. But that is hard to come by.

Do you think teaching commands to a Fairbanks (trail) leader would tend to hurt him?

No. I think a Fairbanks leader would be improved if you could teach him his commands.

Why do some dogs like it better in lead and get shook when they are put back and others like it better in back and get shook when they are put up front?

The reason a leader gets shook when he gets put back is because he is usually trying to stay out in the front. All of a sudden he finds himself maybe one notch back. He doesn't like the idea. But if you give him a little time he gets used to it.

The only reason a dog would get shook when he is put up front is because the dog can't take it out there. Some of the dogs, their minds are not as strong as others.

When you are getting just about the best a dog has got, your whole team has got, they are really under a lot of pressure. When you figure the pressure on that team, you can figure the pressure on those leaders that are stringing those dogs out. That is really a lot of pressure for an animal. Some of the leaders can't take the pressure that is put on them. I haven't seen many animals that could take that kind of pressure from a really high-powered team. That is the reason maybe the first five teams in any race are having a lot of trouble, but they are still winning the race because they are getting the best their animals can give.

In the last three years I have had a lot of trouble with leaders. Ever since I have hit this top speed that an animal can take, I've had trouble coming by leaders that would stay out in front of them. Maybe in five races I have gone through eight leaders. Or I have gone through as many as five different leaders in a single race. When a dog is doing the best he can, he couldn't take the pressure from the crowd. And he couldn't take the pressure you are asking of him. All these little things combined will break a dog's mind and he is going to take you off the trail. About all you could do then is just talk happily to the dogs and try to keep them going.

Have you ever seen your father train a lead dog differently from the way you do it?

My dad must have been a really top dog man. When we were out running the trapline I have seen him turn a whole team of 15 dogs loose. Sometimes a stream bank on the trail was so steep he couldn't see any way of keeping the sled off the dogs if he was to go down that bank while the dogs were hooked up on it. So he would turn the whole team loose and tell them "Get up" and they would take off down the bank. When they got to the bottom he would give a command, and the leader would turn off into the deep snow. When the leader had the whole team off the trail, then the dog would stop, and the whole team would naturally have to stop. My dad would just take the sled down and hook his team back up to his sled.

It sounds easy. I don't know how they do this kind of training. I've never done this kind of training. The way it looked to me — I was just a kid then — it looked to me like it was done all by this one dog. It was all done by voice command.

What sort of a lead dog training course do you use?

I have trails with Ys in them. I don't go the same direction every time. I maybe make a right turn one time and a left turn the next time, or I go right two times, or which ever way I feel like doing it. This is where my command teaching comes in.

How do you train a new leader?

Usually I use an old leader in double lead with a new one to train the new leader to stay out front and to teach him his commands.

You could train a leader without an old leader, but this would take a lot of time. When you are training a leader like this, you have to have full control of your team at all times. If you have a Y in the trail, you lead your dog to which ever way you want to go, gee or haw. I get ahold of him by the neck and give him the command as I lead him over. This is a slow way to train a dog to gee and haw. But I've done this before, and I've come up with some good command leaders.

I've trained leaders with a choke chain the same way you would train an obedience dog. I've trained the leader on foot by running with him and giving him his commands and jerking on the choke chain. That's another slow process thing.

Actually, the best and fastest way to go about it is with an old leader that knows his commands real well. The new dog will pick it up faster if he sees the old leader doing it.

Do you work on a dog until he knows gee before you start him on haw, or do you teach both together?

Usually I just go ahead and teach both together. Never try to do too much in one day. If you are not using an old leader, and you are stopping your dogs and walking up to give them the commands, or you are pulling them by a chain, this could get old for the dog just like it gets old for you.

How long does it take you to train a leader to know gee and haw?

That's hard to say, really. With some dogs it comes faster than with others. Say in a month a dog would know gee and haw. Now I say a month; it could take longer. The dog would know his gee and haw, but that don't mean he is going to do it. As time goes by he gets better at it. It takes at least two years, or more, before the dog is sharp at it.

Training a lead dog you got to be careful. If you start

pushing him, if you demand too much, then you are maybe going to ruin a leader that was coming along good. Like when you give him a command, instead of doing it he will just get all shook up or something. I've done this before. I've been coming up with some very good gee-haw leaders, and then I pushed them too fast and wound up with nothing in the end.

Do you expect your leaders to hold the line out?

This would save you a lot of trouble if you don't have any help around, especially when you are training a bunch of pups. But I don't work too hard on having my leaders hold the line out. I just keep putting them out easy and talking to them. Maybe I would slap them in the seat and tell them to stay out, but I never whip my dogs in the yard to make them hold the line out. I have done it before, but I believe it was a mistake.

If somebody is around, I have them hold the line out.

I can have the line tied ahead, too. I put my leader in last. When I got him hooked up, I unsnap the line that is holding the dogs out and start going back to the sled. If the leader starts coming back toward me — usually the young leaders would do this — he has to be taught to hold the line out until I get back to the sled.

A few years ago I used to hook my leaders up first and have my leaders hold that line until I got the whole team hooked up. But then I learned in the last few years that when you are doing this, you are actually demanding too much from those leaders. So if you hook up your leaders last and just do nothing but have them hold that line out until you get back to the sled, that is good enough. Having them hold the team out for the whole time you hook up is too much.

Does it work to put a leader who is temporarily not making the grade back further in the team, or should you just leave him in the lot?

If it is a dog that doesn't want to do it — not sick, but just lazy — then it would pay to move him back and give him an education that way instead of whipping him. Every time you whip a dog you are breaking down his spirit. When you move a lead dog or a swing dog back, it serves the same purpose as a whipping.

If this dog has got it at all, when he is moved out of lead he is going to try to pick his position back up. A few runs like this and then you could move him into lead again. If this don't work, then I'd go to the whip. But I'd try moving him back first.

If he is sick, you would have to leave him home.

What do you do when your leaders bolt down the wrong trail?

I just try to stop the team as quick as I could — I get pretty good at throwing the snow hook around a tree — and then I turn the leaders around and head back the right way. I don't do no whipping or anything like that.

Do you ever want anyone else to correct your lead dog?

I have never let anybody else correct my lead dog. I would rather do all my training myself. I don't think you should ever let anyone straighten your leader out for you by giving him a whipping or anything like that.

I have heard of where a dog bolted all the time, and so the musher stationed somebody down where the dog bolted to give him a whipping. I don't think that is very good. I wouldn't go that route.

George, why do you always sell your good leaders?

Hmmm. Well, the only reason is for the money I get for the dogs I sell. To keep the kind of team I got right now takes quite a bit of money, even with a good sponsor. Being a working man and working only four and a half months out of a year, I couldn't afford to spend any money I make working for wages on dogs. So actually my kennel has got to be making money or at least breaking even. If it starts losing money, then I couldn't afford to keep it. That's the reason I sell my good leaders, and sell a lot of other good dogs, too. That's the answer right there.

PASSING

How do you train your leaders to pass?

I get somebody else up here in the village to drive half of my team. I start this other musher ahead of me and I want to catch him, so I don't hook up too many dogs with him. Maybe I catch him a mile and a half out. I want him to stop and hold his dogs. I want him on the left side of the trail so I can get a gee pass.

A lot of times the leaders, or even the dogs behind, will try to hook the dogs they are passing with their heads. Then they get tangled up in their lines. Usually these dogs know they are doing something I don't like, but they are just looking for a way of stopping with that team. I whip the dogs when they do this. I work at my leaders until they go by as fast as they can without monkeying around with the other dogs.

After they pass, I teach them to pick it up. If I say "Get up!" and they don't pick it up right, or if they start looking back at the other dogs, then I whip them for it.

The other driver would have a pair of my leaders and I would have a pair, so then I'd let him take my team and I'd repass him. I just keep doing this back and forth until I got both halves of my team passing the way I want them to pass.

Actually this works out pretty good. If you teach your leader to pass fast and pick it up after he passes, then this becomes a habit with him. Then when you start to race and your team passes, they pick it up real fast.

Do you prefer your dogs to pass on one particular side? If so, which one?

In dog mushing it should be a uniform thing to pass on the right-hand side. By that I mean the gee side. If you are overtaking a team and you call "Gee," the lead dog goes to the right. If you are passing head on and call "Gee," the leader goes to the right and both teams miss each other.

I remember when everyone else had dogs here in Huslia that we always used to pass on the right-hand side whether it was head on or going the same direction. We never had any tangles using just this one side. But in the racing circuit, you never know what side you are going to get a pass.

Do you command your lead dog which side to pass, or do you just let him choose?

I command him what side to pass. It is up to you to see which side is best, so you should be the one to tell him which side to pass on.

How do you teach a new lead dog to pass?

I have a double lead, a new dog and one of my older leaders. My older leader naturally wants to go by real fast. If the new dog drags back too much or messes up the team, then there is hardly any way to get around giving him a whipping. Remember, this whipping doesn't hurt this dog any more than a good hard jerk on a choke chain hurts an obedience dog. You got to have some way to get across to him what you want him to do.

What is the best method of passing head on?

Up here we usually pass each other on the gee side. If we can't do it, we give the command for which side looks best at the moment. One of us hollers the command, and both leaders pick it up.

A lot of these trails up here are say 20 inches wide, and a lot of guys up here are really good. Maybe they are driving five or six dogs. We are coming head on, and they have plenty of time to see that I am coming with my big string of dogs. They usually stop then and get ahold of their dogs. I don't know how this came about. I've never had a bunch of fighters or anything, but I've always appreciated this. This has always eliminated all the trouble. I don't think I could remember any time up here where I got in a good mess in passing.

When I am passing a team I don't know, I never pass it too fast. The idea is that I want to be able to stop in a hurry if one of those dogs reaches out and grabs one of mine. If the dog has ahold of one of yours and you can stop, then it is just a bite. But if you are going fast, then a big hunk of skin will be torn off. I had this happen to me once. So much skin got torn off one of my dogs that I had to shoot him. So I don't pass head on fast.

Now passing when you are overtaking a team is different. The dogs aren't looking yours right in the face, and they aren't so apt to bite. But when they see a team of dogs coming at them head on, something happens in their mind.

Do you have much trouble with tangles when you are passing during a race?

Not really. I started racing in 1958. Since that time I could only remember two times that I really got messed up. But those were good ones then.

The first one was in Fairbanks. I knew I was going to pass this guy — I forget who it was — and so I went to him before the race and had it all straightened out what he was going to do. So when I caught him in the race, I don't know what happened to him, but he went to the wrong side of the trail just as I started to go by. A real pile-up.

The second one was — do you remember that guy, his name was Stevens or something, who got in the '68 Rendez-vous? He was inexperienced — never been in a race before apparently. This was five miles out the first day. I spotted him ahead of me in the clear. We were coming to a wooded area, and by the time we got there I was right on his heels. But I didn't say nothing because I'd been on that trail before with a snowgo and it's really crooked through there. I didn't want to try to pass him, and he didn't know I was back there.

God dang it, son of a gun! We were about half way through the woods and I couldn't see him because it was so crooked in there. He stopped on a right-hand turn — a really sharp turn — and when my dogs came around the corner there was no place they could go, so they went straight out into the woods. God, I had a mess in there. I was so mad at this guy. I went out there to work with my dogs and he was holding my sled, and I was standing there arguing with him. And then it came to me, "I'm supposed to be racing, not arguing with this guy."

(Jim Steven's version of the incident went something like this:

"There I was out in the woods minding my own business, and I stopped to undo a little tangle. I heard a shout and looked up just in time to see everything hit the fan. I didn't know any teams were around. I never would have done anything on purpose to mess anybody up, particularly not George – of all people. Wow, did he ever cuss me out!" Ed.)

STOPPING

How do you get your team to obey "Whoa?"

I hardly ever have to work on this. Early in the season when I'm stopping a lot I just use this word whenever I stop, and it just comes natural to them that this "whoa" means stop. But then again, I don't have them trained that good on it.

Do you ever stop your dogs during a run just for a morale builder?

In the fall it seems like I am forever pressed for time, but I try to do it at least half the time I go out. I just stop for a breather, and I try to build their morale up. I go out there and I pet them and I play with them.

After I get done with my heavy training in December, I make it a point to stop on the trail and pet the dogs. When you do this, then their confidence would come back to them, and they won't try to pull your brake off every time you stop. In December stopping means somebody is going to get a whipping. In January stopping means everybody is going to get petted.

Do you ever teach your dogs to stay?

When I stop and am working on the dogs I use the word "stay." I use a tone of voice like I really want them to stay, and usually they do. Better than 75 percent of the time they stay while I am working on them. That other 25 percent of the time they pull the hook out before I get finished.

The thing I do when it doesn't look like my hook is going to hold very good is I never move around fast in my dog team. Whenever I am stopped on the trail I never get in a big rush. I take my time.

I don't train my dogs to stay without setting the snow hook. Even with it set, I'm not going to go off and leave them. If I did, I wouldn't have a team. I don't train my dogs to stay like that. I train my dogs only one way, and that is to go forward.

Now if you aren't racing but are just using your dogs for work, it can be pretty handy if your leader knows how to stop and stay. My mother tells the story of one time when she was out with the team hauling a big load. My brother Steve was real little then and she had him in the sled too. When she was stopped on the trail, the dogs broke the big ring on the sled and took off. This leader — actually it was my dad's leader; his name was Pal — she couldn't tell him to turn off so she yelled "Whoa!" at him. You know, this leader threw himself down and just lay there and the rest of the dogs kept dragging him. My mother caught up with them about a mile down the trail. She turned them around, but she couldn't hang on to them. Just a loose team, you know — I think 11 dogs — so she had to let them go heading towards the sled. Steve was pretty small and just his head was sticking out of the sled as this leader came by. So he told this leader "Whoa!" and the dog stopped. The team was right there when my mother got back. So she tied them back on to the sled and turned them around again and came on home.

LOAFERS

How do you get a dog to lope instead of trot after the first burst of speed?

When you are starting training in the fall and going real short miles, the team always starts out real fast. When the team is still going pretty good and before any dog breaks into a trot, you stop. When you take off again, they are going wide open. Say your track is four miles and you stop pretty often during that four miles. Even if you stop at three and a half miles, after that far, the dogs will start running when you pull the hook. When they are tough enough so that they can go that four miles loping all the way, then you step up the distance.

When you keep doing this, these dogs are learning how to lope fast. It is being built into them.

A leader sets a pace, but not as fast as the team is capable of going. How do you get him to pick it up?

If the dog has got it, if for that first mile he could really put out, really motor, and say you had four more miles to go, there is no reason in the world why he shouldn't give it to you. Like say his name is Ring. If I say, "Ring, get up!" he knows I want more. If he doesn't do it, and if I give this command three or four more times and he still doesn't do it, I use my whip on him. This teaches him to give me what he has got. You can't do this every day though because after a while the dog gets tired of it.

You got to be sure you give your leader a word of praise after he picks it up, or any time he takes a good command.

How do you make a team run up a hill that you know they can make but they think they cannot, or are not willing to try?

You are doing all the thinking. They are going to make that hill at what speed you know they can make it. If they quit, then you have got to force them into it, and that is actually whipping the dogs and making them do it.

What about a dog that always keeps a tight line but you know is letting the other dogs pull for him?

If he has got it and is just putting something over on you, you should get it out of him. You should force him to give it to you. But if he doesn't have it, you might as well forget him.

How do you train a dog to respond to a jingler?

I have this jingler right on the whip when I am training. The jingler and the whip become one thing to him, so when he hears the jingler it reminds him of the whip.

You have six dogs that run well right under the whip. They are smart. If out of reach, they slack off. Do you have any way of reaching the four that are not at wheel?

Any time you have to swing a whip at a dog to make him work, even a wheel dog, you might as well get rid of that dog right now. Any time you swing that whip, you are making the whole team work, if they are trained at all.

When I am training, I never pop my whip behind my sled. The only time that whip comes out is when a dog is going to get a whipping.

When you are in a race with a trained team, that whip should never have to come out. Just the tone of your voice after the team is trained should be all that is doing it. Unless you are in a 25 mile race like the Anchorage race where maybe you have to run on concrete the last two miles. Maybe you have to run that last two miles on nothing but fear and guts. Then you could take your whip out. But otherwise that whip should stay in the bag.

BAD HABITS

What do you do about a bolting leader?

Lead him back on the track and hope he makes the next turn. Or change leaders.

Some of them are so bull-headed that you can't beat them. They know they are being contrary but whipping just makes them worse. The message doesn't get through to them that way. Then there are others that do get the message. It registers, "Well, if I bolt again I'll get...." It all depends on the dog. You got to be able to see that for yourself.

What do you do about a leader that turns around on you?

Actually there isn't very much you could do about this. Say you took a dog out today and he turned around on you, and you gave him a whipping for it. Then tomorrow you took him out and he turned around on you again. Once he got that team turned around, he is really going wild to get that team home because he knows that he got a whipping for turning them around yesterday.

So the best thing you could do when he does turn around on you is just turn him right back again easy, and try to get him going past that point. That's the best method. It just don't pay to whip a dog for turning around.

How do you cure a dog from chewing up his harness or line as you are hooking up?

I just try to keep an eye on him. I always try to keep my dogs in a good mood before I start out so all I do is slap them or something, but I never lay a whip on them or anything of that sort.

I have this stake chain right next to where my towline is stretched out. As I harness the dogs, I snap them to it before they go on the line. That way I can keep a pretty good watch on everybody all at once.

What do you do about a swing dog that gets stubborn and pulls the leader down the wrong trail?

This dog should be further back in the team where he can't pull the lead dog around. Actually, any dog that you think will pull that leader around should be further back in the team.

How do you keep a dog from biting snow?

I water my dogs first thing in the morning before I start running them.

I find that squirting lemon juice in their mouth right before the run works too. They really hate that stuff. This was taught to me quite a few years ago by somebody. I don't know why it is so, but when you squirt this lemon juice in their mouth, they seem to give up biting snow. (Use artificial lemon juice in a plastic, lemon-shaped container. Ed.)

What do you do about a leader who stops to relieve himself?

When I am starting a leader and he does this, I give him a whipping every time he does it. Pretty soon he is doing it on the fly. When he is trained to pick it up, I could just call his name and he will do it on the fly.

Do you try to make the dogs relieve themselves before the race?

No, I don't bother. I train all my dogs earlier to do this on the fly.

How do you break a fighter of the habit?

I have had fighters on my team when the dogs were hitting their peak. This is when you will find that the whole team is ready to fight. I have talked to some coaches of football teams, and they say that men are the same way. When men are at their peak, they feel like fighting too.

I have noticed some dogs in other teams that snap at my team as they are going by. Usually my dogs are running right by and a dog in somebody else's team would snap at one of my dogs and take a great big chunk off of him. I've noticed this in some really good teams here in Alaska.

If one of my dogs did that, I sure would lay the leather on him to cut it out, to break him of the habit. I really would work that dog over.

Why are some young dogs afraid of speed and running down hill?

The reason is because on the first couple of runs you probably took them down a hill too fast. Or you just went too fast. On that first run you have to be pretty careful that these dogs don't get scared.

What do you do about older dogs that won't run down hill?

I don't waste time on them. I get rid of them.

What would you do about a dog that pulls out to the side and makes the gangline look like a snake?

I've never had this problem. But I would say that if you could just keep changing the sides on him you might work him out of it. You know, switch him from left to right and right to left.

How do you make a dog that has gone sour happy again?

You can stop and go out and pet them like I do after I finish with my heavy training. Another way is to lay them up. Usually when a dog team goes sour it is because they have had too much training.

Another thing is maybe you are running on just one trail. Putting them on a new trail will make a lot of difference to the whole team. They get tired of just one trail when you run them on it steadily.

RIDING THE SLED

Back in the old days before snow travelers, the trails weren't like the way they are now. Now we got 20" wide trails and it's all hard and packed. Back then all there was was a runner track. In order for dogs to be able to pull a big load, that sled had to be right on that runner track all the time. And the only way you are going to keep it on there is if you steer from the front.

So they tied a pole on the front of the sled on the right-hand side. That's why they called it a gee-pole. The driver was on a pair of skis in front of the sled hanging on to the gee-pole, using it to steer the sled.

For a long time nobody had enough sense to run a line from that pair of skis to the towline. Any time you had to get off your skis, they stayed behind, like if nobody was helping you and you were going down a bank and had to jump off your skis and grab the back end of the sled and hold the brake. After you got the sled down, you had to go back after your skis. Finally some guy got the idea of tying the skis to the towline so when you had to jump off, the skis would drag along in pretty near the same position.

This wasn't so long ago either because my mother told me she has used a gee-pole with skis that weren't attached.

You can't really steer a sled. All you could do is kick it

around the best you can. I use my heel for this. I use my left heel for a left-hand turn and my right heel for a right-hand turn. I drag my heel on the inside of the runner. You never want to take a chance with your toe on the outside.

I always twist my sled going around a turn. Like if I'm making a right-hand turn, I twist the front end of the sled to the right. And I'll be leaning way over to the right-hand side on a right-hand corner. Then I got all my weight on the right-hand runner, too. I always keep lower down around the turns; I'm not standing up straight.

I probably use my arms more than other drivers because I'm cracking the back stanchion of the sled all the time. Going into turns I balance with my arms and I'm bending the sled. Then when I hit the corner there's a jar on my arms, and I think that's what causes the crack. But even though I crack the sled, I never jerk my dogs around turns.

If you come to a really sharp corner where the trail comes so close to a tree that you are afraid the dogs will pull the sled into it, just as the wheel dogs are going around the corner — but before the sled has started to turn — give a strong pedal to shoot the sled beyond the tree. Then when the sled turns, it will turn sharp, but it will miss the tree. You will jerk your dogs a little by doing this, but not as much as if you hit the tree.

When I want to slow the team down, I usually drag either one or both heels depending on how much I want to slow down. Dragging just one heel won't turn the sled as long as the dogs aren't turning it too. I only use my brake if it's really necessary, like I want to stop or something.

Remember I told you that everybody in Anchorage on the training trail there hardly ever use their brake? They got to be using their heels. They don't ruin the trail that way. With your brake you could ruin a dog trail.

My best riding position, where I feel most comfortable at and most stable, is leaning over the sled. I'd do anything to try to keep from tipping over. Going around corners I get my weight even lower by leaning farther over the handle bar.

"Another place where it's good to get off and run..." Fourth Avenue at the end of the 1970 Rendezvous.

(photo by Maxine Vehlow)

"...swing your foot far enough behind you..." 1969 Rendezvous.

(photo by Maxine Vehlow)

What some of the guys that are fast enough do when they don't want to turn over is they hold on to the handle bar and run around bad corners. This takes the strain off the wheel dogs, too. (I've seen Beattus Moses of Allakaket do this 200 yards out of the chute at the Tudor Track in Anchorage, before they cut out that corner. Ed.) And they do it at real rough places in the track, like going from a road over a snow berm to get on to a training trail. A sled doesn't turn over when there isn't any weight on it.

Another place where it's good to get off and run is when the course goes over bare pavement. Less drag on the sled. If it's a long distance on pavement, you run alongside the sled and pull it towards you so that the sled is riding on the edge of only one runner.

It is good to do this any time when you are coming in to the finish line and need to pick up a second or two, like when two teams are coming in neck and neck and you want to be first across. You figure how much strength you have left. Then you get off and run and tip the sled over so that the dogs have hardly any weight to pull across that line.

I've been asked about pumping. Pumping the sled is not really pushing the sled, it is mostly just taking your weight off it. Unless maybe you got 100 yards to go before the finish line, then you could push the sled with one leg. But more than that a person couldn't take.

There aren't too many of us that can pedal all the time, but if we could help a little bit now and then, anything would help. One place you can pump is like when you are going to hit a bump. If you pump right at the bottom of the bump to push the sled over it, that will save the team from getting jerked.

When you are pumping, you got to make sure you don't jerk the lines. That is a thing you want to keep away from at all times. It is better not to pump at all than to jerk the team.

To get the most out of each pump, you got to be sure that you swing your foot far enough behind you. Even when your foot is in the air, it seems to be pushing the sled.

TRAILS

Do you prefer to run on just one trail, or do you run on different trails so that the dogs don't get bored?

My training in Huslia is done on just one trail because all the other trails are so rough because of snow travelers. I keep one trail as my training trail and the villagers respect it. It is not chewed up by snow travelers. October, November, December — the dogs run on that same trail. Sure they get bored. That's how come they act so lazy, not really eager to run. But then they don't get hurt either. They get to know every hole. The main thing is to try to keep from hurting dogs as much as you can. I figure I will keep going like this until I get out of here. When I can truck my dogs, then I can train on a new trail.

How do you pack your trail?

Every snowfall I'm on that trail. I run my dogs on it first thing in the morning, and then I go out with my snowgo in the evening. I drag a big tire on the trail to sort of smooth it out. The tire makes it wide, too. But the dogs pack the trail better than just a snowgo can.

Some guys don't drive dogs, only snowgos. Their trail never really packs. Maybe they miss a couple of snowfalls. Their trail is all right for snowgos, but not for dogs. You run it two times with a dog team and the dogs start punching through.

So I'm packing my trail all winter with the dogs, and there's no chance of falling through. Every snowfall.

Some drivers like to train in deep snow so that their dogs don't get hurt. Others prefer hard packed roads. Would you comment on training on different types of snow?

I don't mind training on a trail that has four or five inches of loose snow on top of a hard packed trail. I think that is good training there. It gives the dogs a good workout. A little bit of soft snow on top seems to be easier on them too.

If the trail is just hard packed and not smooth, like bumps from snowgos, the dogs are not going to be able to hit every bump just the way they want to, especially if they are going wide open. On training trails like this, I always take it easy because a rough trail makes for an unbalanced dog.

Some of the race tracks are not put in early enough. If a race track is not packed all the way down, usually it gets punchy. It is okay for the first three or four guys, then you get more teams on there and it starts punching up. On trails like this where the dogs are trying their best and are losing their footing and punching through every time they jump, you have a chance of crippling dogs. If the going is real rough, I slow them down. I figure we could always make it up. In a really short race you couldn't make it up, but in a race of 15 or 16 miles or more you could slow your dogs down for half a mile. You might be saving a dog.

Do you sometimes look for hill training? Would you train differently if you lived in the mountains?

No, I don't look for hill training. I don't think there is any such thing as training for hills or for flat going or for a foot of snow or hard packed trails. I don't train differently for any of those conditions. It all boils back down to the same thing, how good you can get your dogs to respond to you when you ask for more speed, no matter what kind of going you got.

But there is just so much a dog can do. In a race you know that the next guy is having as much trouble as you are. There is no way in the world he is going to keep his dogs going steady in six inches of snow for 20 miles. Even if his dogs are as tough as yours, if you can get a better response out of yours, then you are going to beat him.

LAME DOGS

Do you believe that speed lames dogs?

Yes, speed lames dogs. Usually how dogs go lame is when they are wide open and they don't have no pull on their backline. There is nothing for them to balance with. They learn to balance with that harness when they are running just their natural run, but when they hit their top speed, that sled is going so fast it slacks up the line. If I am going downhill, I try to keep that backline tight on all the dogs. Or uphill. Or on level ground. Anywhere I try to keep all the lines tight so the dogs have something to balance with. Usually the dogs don't go lame then.

Maybe you got one starting out slow. That one could very easily get hurt if he doesn't have any pull on his backline and is being pulled by his neckline. Then he is hitting too hard on his front quarters. That could very easily hurt him. So these things you try to avoid.

I have always managed to keep my team together pretty good. A lot of times I would end up a three day race with a 13 dog team. This year I had 15 dogs finish Rendezvous. This gives me an advantage over the guys who are pretty short on dogs. The lowest I have ever got on dogs was last year at Tok. The last day I ran with nine dogs. So except for last year, my dog team really holds together well.

Do any of your lame dogs ever make it back into the team that same year?

If I cripple some dogs after they are tough, like after December when my dogs are as tough as they will ever get all winter, then these dogs have a chance of coming back.

If they went lame in November when they still have a way to go before they get tough, I try to rush the dogs back into work so they can keep up with the rest of the team — which isn't good for them.

But if the dogs get crippled earlier than that, usually they are just out for the winter. There is no way in the world I could bring them up, get them as tough as the rest of the team. So I don't even bring them into town with me. I just leave them home.

How do you bring back a lame dog?

When a dog is going lame, you could usually spot it roughly three runs before he actually goes lame on you. You could see that he is hurting when he is running. It just shows very slightly at first. If you could spot this, then you have got it made. But usually the first time people spot this is when he is too far gone already. He has pulled a muscle bad, maybe carrying one leg.

When I first spot this, I give them a shot of Depo-Medrol. I just tie them up and leave them on the chain for three days. If I catch this early enough, usually within three days they are as good as new.

If I miss that point where they are first hurting, the next time I run them I may have gone too far. They may have gotten hurt too bad by then. I still give them a shot of Depo-Medrol, but then I don't run them with the team anymore.

When one of my truckload of dogs goes lame, I give him a shot of Depo-Medrol, and then I walk the dog a lot. Actually, the handler walks the dog. Like last year was a bad year, and just before the race I had four dogs walking around keeping limber.

If I run these dogs to keep them limber, I do it with a three dog team. They aren't really running, just walking or trotting, just getting exercise so they don't get soft. I don't do this every day, and I make them pull a little weight so they don't run free.

I rub them, too, especially during the race. Maybe I will have eight dogs in the house the morning of the race, just rubbing them. I use Absorbine Junior cut down with water.

I check my dogs over every morning after I get up. I go out with a pail of water about eight o'clock. The dogs are inside the truck so I let them out. That is when you can spot who is stiff. If the dogs are really good, they could run. They don't get worse during the race. When they get heated up they don't seem to feel it. Usually it takes two or three miles and these dogs are just as limber as the rest. But it has to be a tough, hard-headed dog. It can't be a weak dog. Just because he is hurting a little it can't be one who says, "To heck with it. I'm not going to run this morning." He just keeps going, and pretty soon he is fitting in with the rest of the team.

I had so many lame dogs last year at the North American that if I was going to drop every one of them I might as well have called it quits. But as it was, I started with 12 dogs. Out of those 12, when I took them out of their boxes in the morning, better than half of them were lame and stiff. But they all made it except one. One of them had to come in in the basket. And actually they came in pretty good. (Second. Ed.)

Do you use a dog that has gone lame one year again the next year?

Yes. Sometimes the reason they go lame is maybe one dog would run better if he was a little heavier, or maybe you should take a little weight off of him. I've run dogs that have gone lame two years in a row, and then I have put more weight on them or taken a little off. I try both ways. Then the next year they don't go lame.

I've had dogs that ran for three or four years and never got hurt, and I'd say, "This dog is hard as rocks." And then he would come up lame. I've run dogs from the time they were pups until they were too old to run anymore, and they never got hurt. But you never know, any dog can get hurt.

The reason some of us keep running a dog that we know goes lame easily is because this dog is a top notch dog, and they are hard to find. Even if we have one that goes lame year after year, we run them and just hope for the best. That is what it boils right down to.

HEALTH

When is it too cold to run dogs?

I never heard of anyone going out on the trapline and saying, "Well, it was 40 below for a month so I stayed in my cabin for the whole month." People have lived in the sticks up north for years. When they ran out of meat they didn't say, "Well, it's too cold to go out and catch a moose." They went out and caught a moose. So who's to say when it's too cold to run dogs.

It's not necessary to go out in weather like that anymore though. Those days are past. If it's too cold for me, I stay in. Like if it's 30 below, unless it's a race, I don't go out. If I go out to train in about 20 below, then I take it easy. Maybe I would run for five or six miles, and that would be it.

Do you worry about frozen lungs?

I worry about freezing a dog's lungs, but I've never done it. In fact, I've never even seen a dog with frozen lungs.

Do you train your dogs in freezing rain?

It isn't worth taking your dogs out in a freezing rain because you are going to get a crust that will cut their feet up. Usually what I do in weather like that is go out and work on my trail. I try to tear the crust up.

If I do take the team out, it is just to keep them in shape. I don't do any training. I drag a tire to keep them from loping, just hold them down to a trot. If they were running on an icy trail, it would cut their feet up. You'd be finishing your dog team.

Do you have much trouble with frozen feet?

I got a dog here right now with frozen feet; Junior, that's what his trouble is. Maybe it started with just a little bit of blood. Then every time I ran him — the weather has been real cold — it froze a little more. The skin is all split between the toes. A dog with bad frozen feet could even get a split on the pad.

Another thing. Like say I am out in about 20 below and go through a stretch of water — usually up here it's overflow — what I do is I stop right then. I don't keep going at all. I rub snow on the dogs' feet to dry the hair out so their feet won't freeze. You really have to watch for this.

I had a whole team of frozen feet one time. What happened then was I went up to Hughes to borrow dogs from Bill William and William Koyukuk and Henry Peters. They loaned me 16 dogs. I was driving the dogs back to Huslia and the weather turned cold. It got dark, and I went into an overflow and didn't know it so I didn't stop. The next day I found out I had a bunch of frost-bit feet. That was the end of that dog team.

Have you ever used dog boots? If so, what did you use?

I've used boots when I didn't have no other way to go. The idea of the boot would be just so that he don't get soft while his foot is healing. If you are toughening him in, you don't have to run him hard. You could just run him for a long distance. I wouldn't recommend whipping a dog when he has a boot on because you would be making him dig, and then he would have a chance of hurting himself. I've hurt dogs by using boots, but I think the problem was mine.

I've never used boots in a race. I figure that if a dog is so hurt that he can't run without a boot, then there is no sense in running him.

I really don't recommend using boots or anything on a dog's feet because if you put a boot on one foot, he doesn't have the feeling in that foot like he should. It is just like a human. If you took one boot off and started walking around, you would feel uncomfortable. A dog must be the same way. If you put a boot on him it has got to throw him off balance.

(George's dog boots are two pieces of soft leather sewn together like a sock. A string attached near the top ties them on the dog's foot. They don't stay on too well. I know; I've made them for him. Ed.)

Do you ever put grease on your dogs' feet?

No, I've never used grease or anything like that.

What are the standard shots given to village sled dogs?

Usually distemper and rabies.

How many days at a time of just easy running do you think a team could take?

I remember when we were going beaver trapping — there were two months of trapping — our dogs were working doggone near every day of that two months. By the end of the two months we had a really good team. So actually, as long as they are not being worked into the ground and as long as they are in good condition, they could pretty much do that every day.

Between what ages is a dog in his prime?

I think probably the toughest years are between four to six or seven. Right in that age.

What is the average retirement age?

It is really hard to say right now, the way the diet is, the way the race teams are eating. Speaking for my team, the way my dogs are fed right now, I would think the average retirement age would run around eight years. But I got one that is going on 11 years that I am still running.

Do older dogs need fewer miles than young ones to get in condition?

A dog is in his top shape when he is four years old. Anything younger than that does take a few more miles. Some dogs don't take many miles and others take a lot to get them tough. If you have the same dog two years in a row, then you know how much that dog needs. But usually the older dog takes a little less conditioning than the young one.

Should a dog under 18 months old be raced hard?

Truthfully, a guy shouldn't run a dog under 18 months old in a big race. I've run them at 14 months old in a race and they didn't go lame, but my advise would be not to do it. Not because these dogs didn't come through for me, but because I don't believe that a dog is as tough as he is going to get before 18 months. A dog should have two years to grow up and know what it is all about before he is really racing hard.

But I've done it every year. I start working my dogs in the fall when they are about a year old. They just keep coming along and coming along, and pretty soon they are better than maybe half the dogs in my team. When you are up against it and you got the Rendezvous to run and you want a full string of dogs and you had a 14 months old pup in there that was better than eight of your dogs, then there is hardly any way you are going to talk yourself into leaving him home. So I have gone ahead and run them, and I don't think I have ever ruined a dog of that age.

TRAVEL

If you were to travel "outside," how long before the race date would you try to arrive?

I would try to get there at least a week ahead of time. Two weeks would be better yet. It would take me five days to get there, and with all that cramped up space, the dogs are bound to lose some of their toughness. And they should get used to the area, too.

When you are traveling, how often do you let your dogs out?

Twice a day; once in the morning when I water and then in the afternoon when I feed.

Do you have any trouble with your dogs traveling in the truck?

When we first got into town, we had this one young dog, Patches, that was yelling all the time. So we put him on Karen's side of the truck, figuring that she's going to break him of this. We put a rope around his neck so she could jerk on it every time he yelled.

At the first yell she jerked, and the line came loose in her hands. We thought it had come untied, so we stopped to do it up again. Found he had bitten it off. So I tied it on better this time. Son of a gun, just as soon as we shut the door he must've snapped that line off. It was the first jerk; she had nothing! That was the end of his training program. Since then he's yelled half-way across Alaska, all the way through Canada, Minnesota, Wisconsin yesterday, and now he's starting on Michigan.

What do you find that air travel does to the dogs?

What I have noticed in airplane travel, Huslia to Anchorage, is that the change of weather affects the dogs more than anything. Maybe you got fifty below in Huslia. Maybe it is zero in Anchorage. Going from cold to warm really knocks the life out of a dog. Going from warm to cold, it seems like the dogs perk up and feel real good.

How long before the race do you like to be on the race site?

I like to be there about an hour before the race. It makes me feel that much easier when I am right there.

RACE STRATEGY

Some old timers used to carry a fresh dog in the basket on the long distance runs of the late twenties. Have you ever carried a fresh dog part of the way?

There is just one time that I carried a dog from the starting line, and that was in Huslia. When we were just racing with a family team, sometimes it was hard to fill in a dog team. The reason I did it that time was because we had a whole bunch of snow the night before the race. I was running number two, and I figured I was going to catch number one. It was about a 16 mile race. I had this one dog that I knew couldn't make the distance, and I knew I couldn't get any speed with that much fresh snow on the trail. So I figured that as long as I was behind number one I would haul this dog, and once I passed him I would drop the dog off the sled. That way I would have a fresh dog, and I would have a chance of getting away then. It worked out just like I figured in that race, but I wouldn't consider doing it for any of the big races.

If a person was really short of dogs, it might work out under certain conditions. But on a good hard trail I just don't see how it is going to help you. Your team is only going to travel as fast as that bummest dog you got. If it can't make the distance, there has got to be something wrong with it. If you got seven dogs and you want eight, and that eighth can't make it, you'd be better off leaving that eighth dog on the chain. I've heard a saying that more races are won by dogs on the chain than there are in the races.

How do you peak your dogs out for a race?

It all starts back in the fall. You got to take enough time to toughen your dogs and teach them to respond. A couple of weeks before the race you change to attitude runs to bring their morale back up. A day or so before the race you just show them the whip to remind them it's there. And then you go out and do your best to win the race.

Do you get the jitters just before a big race?

I am uptight before the race just like I believe everybody else is. But I try not to show it to my dogs. I try to act just the way I do all the time.

How do you plan your races?

I always have a general idea of how I would like to run a race depending on the distance. If I don't take my dogs around the track, I try to look it over with a snow traveler. I look at the conditions, the bad places, and plan accordingly. I figure I am going to get so much here and so much there. The main thing is to try not to hurt that top dog in your team because top dogs are really hard to come by.

In a two or three day race do you change your dogs around because of the weather?

I take a lot of time to think about the weather and the trail. One dog may be great if the weather is nice, but another might be a better driver if it is snowing and a wind is blowing. Any dog can run on a good trail, but some leaders are tougher than others if the wind has drifted the trail over in the night. I really study my dogs and the

Drawing for position for first day's start, 1970 Rendezvous. Holding the box is Race Marshall Dick Tozier. (photo by Maxine Vehlow)

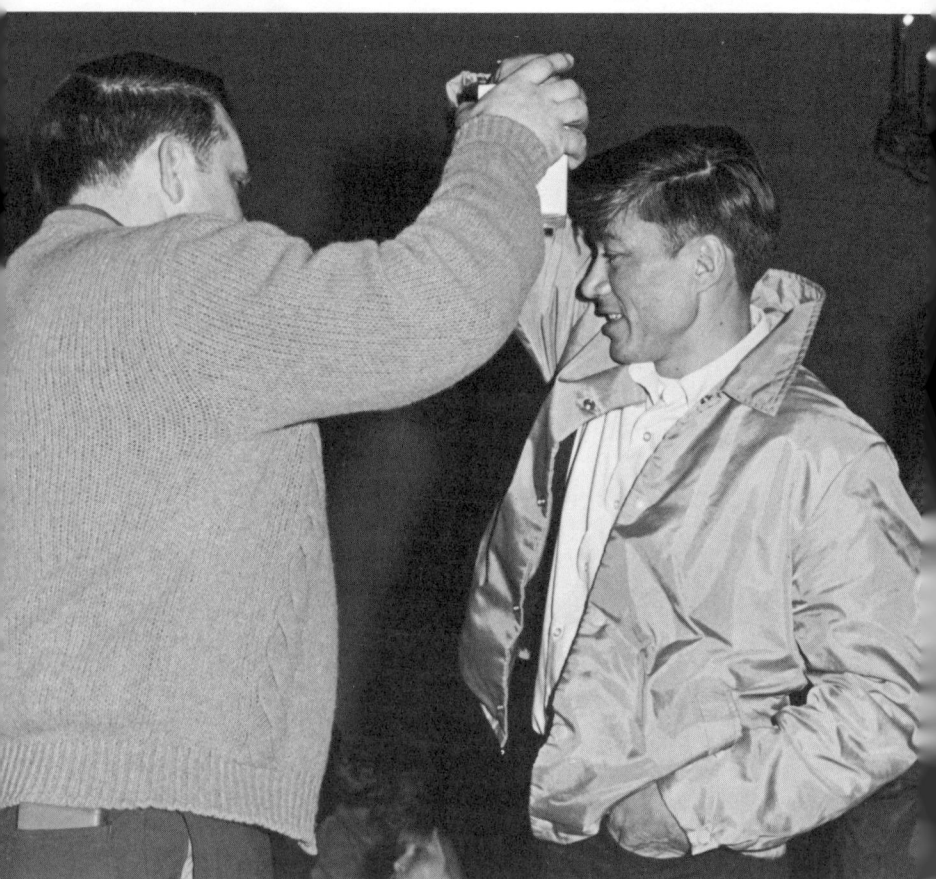

conditions. I always sit down the night before a race with pencil and paper and decide who is going to run where.

If your team is not anxious to run the second or third day of a race, do you do anything to liven them up?

One thing I do is take my team to the starting line without the leader. I have someone else bring the leader along behind on a leash. Then I walk the leader up and down the team before I hitch him in. This helps, particularly if it's a female leader.

Another thing I do is at just about the 30 second count, I stand in front of the whole team and clap my hands softly and talk to the dogs. I walk back easy and get to the sled with about three seconds to go. (The handlers have a fit! Ed.)

Do you have dogs that you use for short races but not for long ones?

I've come up with dogs like that, but it wasn't because I wanted them on my team. Usually I get rid of dogs like that. When I load up my truck, it is with the idea that every one of those dogs can stay with the team for as long as whatever race I am going to run.

Do you have dogs that run only one day?

No. That is not the way I figure it. When I start with a dog I figure he is going to go three days. But sometimes he doesn't. I've made mistakes and had to haul dogs.

There have been times when I know that a dog is only going to help me one day. I know it's all he's got. When I put a dog like that in, it is just because I don't have anything else to put in. My best is already in there, and I figure, "Well, this dog is going to help me a little bit for one day."

How do you know when a dog that has run the course well one day is too tired to make it the next day?

Usually after you finish a race your dogs are all pooped when you come in. But then when you get back to your place and the dogs have been in their box for a little while and you take them out to water, they feel like they want to move around again. Well, you know they have got their

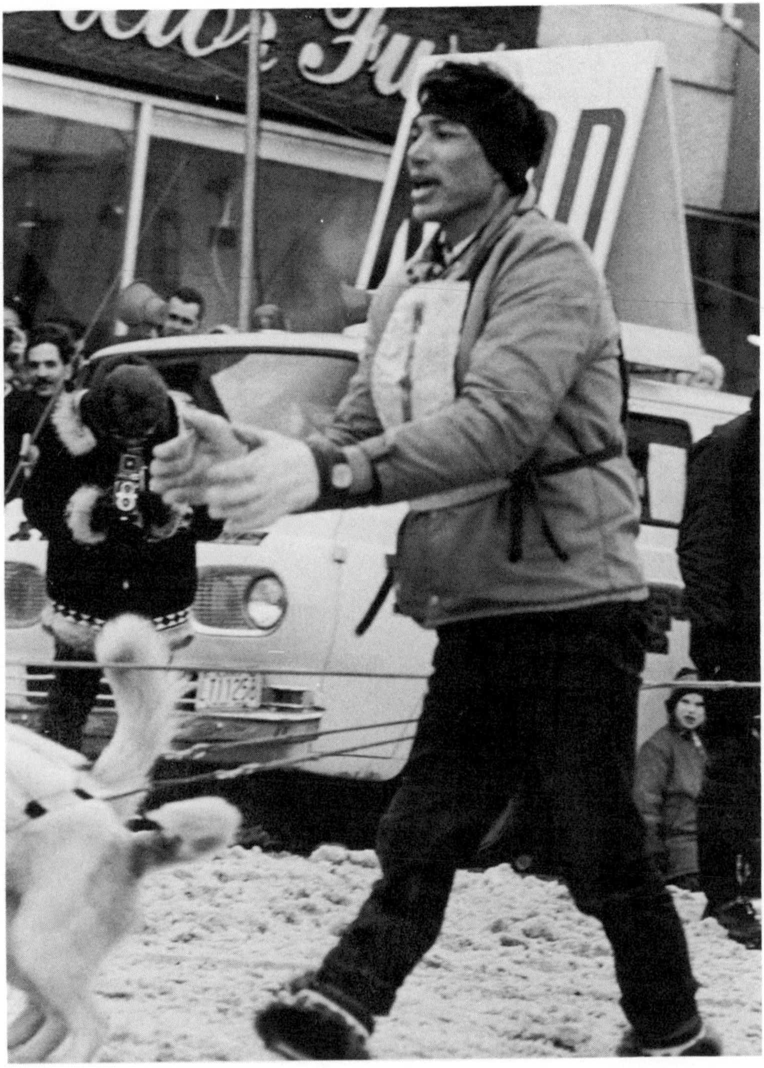

At the starting line, 1970 Rendezvous. Leaders, from left to right, Scotty and Coolie.

(photo by Maxine Vehlow)

strength back. But sometimes I've had a dog that felt like a bucket of water when I started taking him out of his box. That dog is finished. That dog worked his guts out for you today and gave you everything he had, and you aren't going to be able to get nothing out of him tomorrow. You could see that he is acting like he didn't want to move around. When you carry him he is like a rag.

I've made mistakes by talking myself into it. Like I am running short of dogs, and I say I am going to have to run this dog again. I could see this dog was finished, but then I start talking to myself and I say that this dog has never let me down before and I am going to need him tomorrow. By the next day I have got myself believing that this dog wasn't all that tired. It hasn't happened very often to me, but it taught me a lesson.

That is something that a person should really watch. When you get them back to the house, and a dog doesn't look like he could do it the next day, you had better be honest with yourself that he can't do it the next day, whether he did it for three or four years or not. It could mean that there is a dog in the basket on the third day.

If a dog drops because he is tired but not because he is quitting, would you run him again in another race?

Yeah, I would run this dog again if he was a good dog and just worked himself into the ground. If I thought that he could take the next race, then I would run him again.

How would you feel about having another musher race some of your dogs as a training procedure?

I've brought handlers down from the village without any pay at all, so I've let them race just to give them something to do. But I don't think it's a good idea. I don't want any of my dogs hurt by someone else doing something wrong with the team. My truckload of 24 dogs is my team that I'm going to be working with for the winter. I really don't think too much of somebody else running them.

Do you usually ride the brake at the start of a race?

Whenever you let a big string of dogs loose, you have to watch it that the back end doesn't overrun the front end.

Particularly in a race where there is a lot of noise and confusion, the back end is going to get the message that it is time to go before the front end does. So you got to keep the brake on until the leaders get going and get the team strung out. That's why I almost always ride the brake for a ways at the start of a race.

Sometimes the leaders just don't take off good. Everybody else takes off good, but the leaders kind of hang back. Like two years ago in the North American, the leaders hung back for four miles. The first four miles I rode the brake. I didn't want to yell at the dogs because the dogs would start working too hard. I did yell at them finally, and they started working.

I'll talk a little bit here about pulling the leader around.

When you take your team up to the starting line of a race, one thing you want to make sure of is that there is somebody behind that leader holding the line tight. If it is the third day of a three day race, none of the dogs are really anxious to go. Say there are a couple way in the back that don't want to go and are jerking over to the side. You want to keep those dogs from jerking on that leader because every time he feels a jerk on his towline he is getting the message through the towline that there are some dogs back there in the team that don't want to go. He is not anxious to go either, so it puts him just that much more on edge.

So one of the best things you could do in a three day race is have somebody stand between the swing dogs and the leader and keep the pull off that leader's tug. It relieves a lot of tension on the leader, and I think it helps.

Do you pump during training? Do you pump during a race?

I pump during training just so the dogs get used to it. You can't just go out there on race day and start pumping. I have done that in the past, and when I first started doing it, the dogs looked back wondering what the heck was going on back there because they were not used to my pumping. So you have to get them used to it.

During a race, what I try to do is pump right from the start and pump the whole course. A lot of races are won and lost by seconds. If you aren't as good a man as the next guy and can't pump as much, especially if the track is a rough one, then you are losing the race.

How much do you talk to your dogs while you are training or racing?

Well, this all depends. I don't talk to them just to be talking to them. I talk to them because it is necessary. In a race you don't have to talk that much to a well trained team that is going well. Maybe once in a while I just make a little noise to hold their attention. Sometimes I am just playing with them and making them run out of happiness. If they are falling behind, I tell them to get up or whistle at them. Then other times I am really asking for everything.

There are very few words that they understand, so I only talk to them in the language they understand. I don't go using a whole bunch of words that they don't know what I am talking about.

You got to watch the dogs losing interest in the tone of your voice, so you don't use just one tone all the time. You switch back and forth. You use a particular tone of voice for what you want.

You can't yell at your dogs all the time. If you keep yelling at them and yelling at them and they are putting out all they can, then they are going to look for ways to get out of it. I've had dogs do this before. I've gotten in a race and I've caught up a team. My dogs were going at their limit right after they passed the team, and the guy behind me would be driving his dogs. My dogs would be wide open, and maybe the guy sticks with me for two miles just constantly yelling at his dogs. At the end of two miles I could see my dogs were looking for ways to get out of this. They were giving all they had, and yet somebody was yelling at them.

So there is such a thing as talking too much to your dogs. There is a limit to what they could take.

Do you have any comments you would care to make about passing during a race?

What I usually do before a race if I think I am going to pass a guy, is we get together and talk. It is best to talk over something that you think is going to happen on the trail before it happens. It is best to talk over what side you want to pass — I always want a right-hand pass — and the whole works. That way you eliminate all the trouble and maybe gain a couple of seconds. Maybe it would speed you up that much and maybe that is what you won by. And it helped the other guy that much, too. You don't hurt nobody's feelings by doing this. It is just kind of keep each other out of trouble is all it is.

I prefer to have a team that I catch stop. I can get a better pass that way so it saves trouble. If both teams are moving, it is much easier for them to get messed up. I think that if a team gets caught, it is ahead if it can keep the other team from getting messed up. If the team that is passing gets messed up, it costs both teams time.

There are some guys that would stop too soon. Sometimes I would be pulling up on a team and I'd have quite a ways to go yet, and the guy would stop and just stand on his brake and wait for me to catch him. Unless he is going to go out there and hold his dogs as I go by, if he stops too soon his dogs are going to scatter all over the trail and my dogs won't have any place to go. He ought to stop just as I catch him.

Actually, I am pretty careful when I catch a team. I brake my team down to where I am just putting out the same speed that the other team is doing before I try to holler "Trail!" Then that way when his team does stop, his dogs are still strung out and not scattered all over the trail, probably eating snow. So it is a good thing not to stop too soon when you do get caught.

After you have made a pass, you could always figure that you've got that five minutes or a mile which is in most of the rules that I know of in Alaska. So if your dogs need a blow, you could just let them set their own pace for a couple of minutes and let them get their wind back. Then speed them up before the guy behind you hollers "Trail!"

I really think that like say in a 20 mile race, if the guy that started two minutes behind you caught you up at say 14 miles, there is hardly any sense in calling for trail unless he is going very slow. I have noticed a lot of teams in a race keep passing back and forth. Every time you pass a team it takes time. Actually once you get passed, it is better just to kind of pace the guy, to stay behind him. That guy is doing the work you would be doing if you were the one that was out there. If it doesn't look like he could do it, then that would be the time to pass. But if he is doing just as good as you could, let him do the work. I would recommend that. If you could get away with it, let him do the work, and you are gaining by just staying behind.

One point on this passing we should discuss a little bit. I've found out that when you get a team in sight, you should never try to catch it as fast as you can. Just let the dogs do it on their own. Don't push them up there to that musher. If you do, you may be winding your team. You will find that they don't want to pass as much as they do if they just catch up on their own. And once they pass, if they are trained to speed up after they pass, then they can't do this if they are already winded. Where if you let them catch up on their own, after you pass you can tell them to pick it up, and then they naturally are going to pick it up real fast. Then you have a chance of pulling away from that team you caught.

This is good because any time a team sticks right on your heels, that team could work you into the ground. Like say you caught a team at 10 miles in a 25 mile race, and he stuck to your tail for 15 miles. It's easy for his dogs to stick to you because they are chasing. Your dogs have to work harder to stay ahead because they aren't chasing nobody. They won't have anything left at the end of the race. And you've been so busy worrying about this team behind you that you haven't been able to run the race the way you want to. I've had this happen to me before. I've made mistakes by worrying too much about a team right next to me. I'm better off by myself, running my own race.

Now there's things you can figure out for yourself that you can do on the trail that's within the rules – or not even in the rule book — but you could figure them out for yourself. You can pull these things and there's nobody can complain. Because what's their complaint? You can mess a guy up so bad that you could just leave him sitting there. And he hasn't got one complaint. I don't claim to know it all, but I've learned some of these lessons the hard way.

Do you think an 8 dog team can go as fast as a 16 dog team?

When I'm training with an 8 dog team, I expect them to go as fast as a 16 dog team. But I don't expect them to hold their speed mile after mile like a 16 dog team could. If trail conditions and weather are just right, an 8 dog team could compete with a 16 dog team. A dog can run just so fast and that's it, so hooking up more dogs doesn't necessarily mean that the team will go faster.

Do you ever stand for your dogs breaking from a lope into a trot?

Depends on what kind of a race it is. If it is a really tough race, like a real hot day and the trail is poor, there is no way you are going to make that dog team lope the whole track. Just make them run where they can. But then you could figure that the rest of the guys are having the same problem because conditions are so tough. So even if you are trotting, you have a good chance of winning that race.

In a race when do you use your jinglers and when do you use the whip?

In a 20 mile race when you keep asking for it, just the tone of your voice gets old after a while. When you could see that the dogs are stopping paying attention to you, that is where your jinglers come in. Usually you lose the dog's attention when there are a lot of people around. Like at a road crossing, you give them a command and use the jingler at the same time. All you have to do is rattle your jinglers and the whole thing comes back again. The dogs could live with the jingler because it don't make as much noise as that whip. But you don't want to use your jingler too much because it will get old, too.

When you are in a race that whip should never have to

come out. After the team is trained just the tone of your voice and the jinglers should be all that is doing it. Unless maybe the last two miles of the Anchorage race where you are running on concrete and only fear and guts are going to get you across the finish line, then you could use your whip. But otherwise that whip should never come out of the bag.

What do you think of pushing the sled at the end of a race?

I've noticed this in a lot of teams up here. A team is coming in the last couple of miles of a long race. The dogs are just completely pooped, but the musher is still in pretty good shape. That musher is pushing his sled too fast to where the dogs are bunching up. If it is a long way to the finish and you had a dog that could go a little faster than the leader, then it would pay to change them around. But if that is all you got, it is best to just help the dog along but keep them strung out and not try to go any faster than that tired leader can go. Don't bunch them up.

What is pacing a team? How do you do it?

You have got your pace already set, the pace you built into them when you were training in the fall. So there is only one way to go from there, and that is faster.

The dogs will take off wide open for say the first four miles. Then the team would naturally slow down. They would go into their pace. It is best to just let them go. They started out faster than they should have, and they have to slow down to catch their breath. Now if you try to push them when they first start to slow down, then you are going to wind this team.

I let them go at their own pace for say a mile or so before I make them pick it up again. Actually, my team would be going pretty much on their own for say the first six miles.

I always plan on finishing that race with some power, so I speed them up according to that. What I do is speed them up, and then I let them go at their pace. I don't do this very much the first ten miles, but after I pass the ten mile point I really make them run fast for a couple of

"HOW I RUN THE 20 MILE RACE IN FAIRBANKS."

Huslia, Nov. 6, 1970

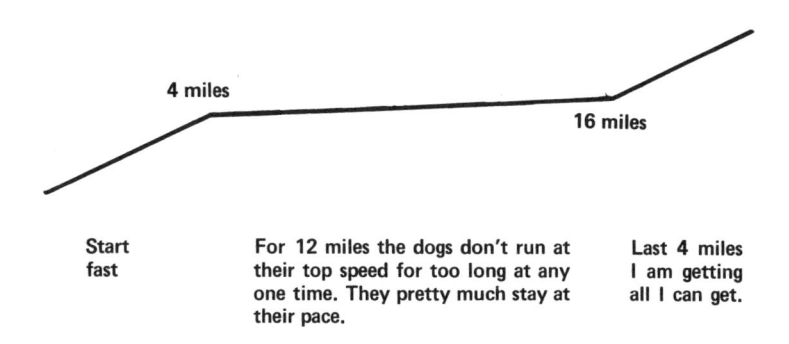

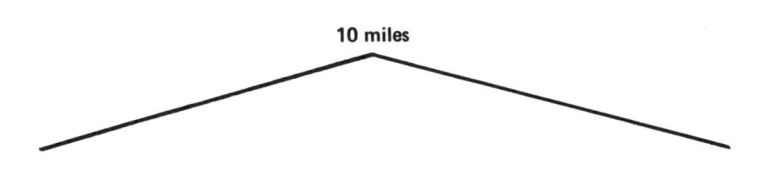

Start fast

4 miles

16 miles

For 12 miles the dogs don't run at their top speed for too long at any one time. They pretty much stay at their pace.

Last 4 miles I am getting all I can get.

10 miles

There are some drivers that do it this way. Their team is winded by 10 miles because he never let up.

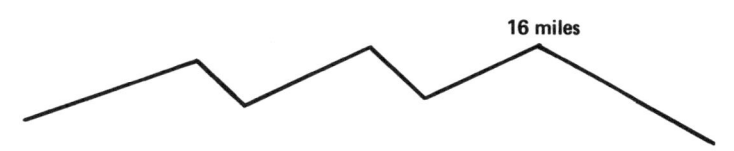

16 miles

A team like this might be ahead at 16 miles, but his team would be winded by 16 miles from not setting a pace but going too fast for a ways and then slowing down too much.

"If I'm pacing myself in a 20 mile race and the last four miles I get into a mess where I have to drag the dogs around, that would really do me in." Crossing the finish line in the 1970 Rendezvous after trouble on Cordova Street.

(photo by Maxine Vehlow)

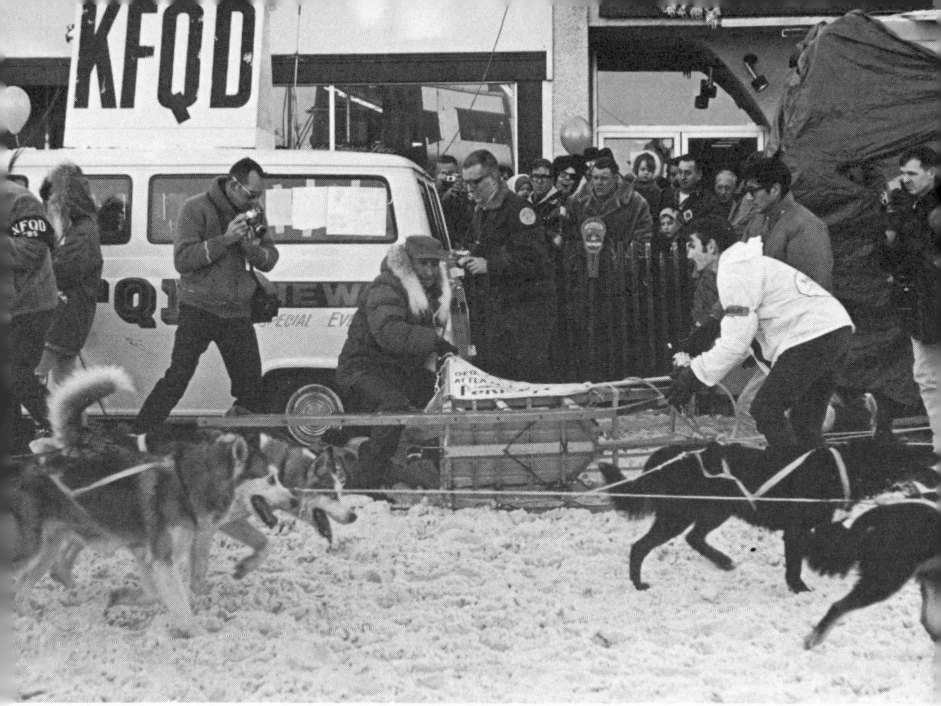
KFQD

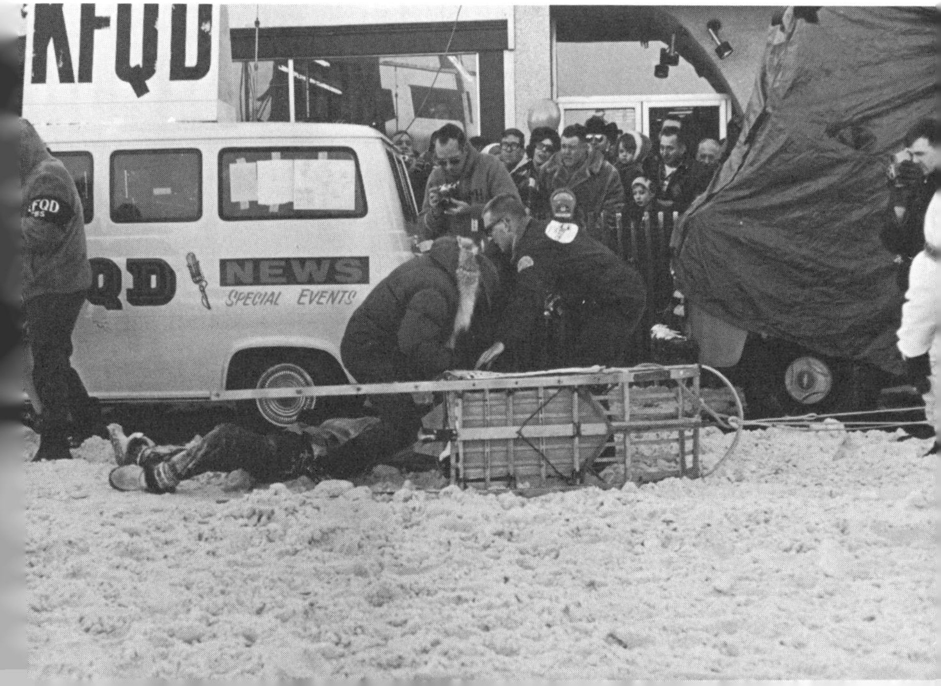
NEWS
SPECIAL EVENTS

miles. Then I let them slow down again. I let them fall into their pace for a couple of miles, and then speed them up again.

From right around the 22 mile point I make them run pretty fast. That last four miles I am still going at a wide open clip. Usually at the end of this race my whole team is completely pooped. They gave me everything they had, whether they won the race or not.

How do you pace yourself during a race?

I do it the same way I pace my dogs. I know how much my dogs could take, so that is what I take out of them. I know how far I can push myself, so that is how much I take out of myself. Of course I may get into unforseen trouble. If I'm pacing myself in a 20 mile race and the last four miles I get into a mess where I have to drag the dogs around, that would really do me in.

I try to pump the whole course. Actually the hardest work on the race track is not the pumping part. It is when you get in trouble. You would be pumping along and pacing yourself. You are figuring you got so much. And then your dogs bolt. Then you are using all this energy right away when you weren't planning on using it. If a guy isn't in shape, then he can't make the race track.

A man who can't handle himself and is not in good physical condition I don't think has got any business running a dog team. Now I have misjudged myself before and been so exhausted that I almost passed out, but these were circumstances I couldn't control. These were not in the big plan when the race started. So it does happen. You make mistakes on yourself, too. But you try to eliminate all this by understanding yourself, understanding how much you can take and what is best for you.

Do you do anything special for your dogs after a race?

You have to show your dogs that you're satisfied with them. I don't necessarily do this right at the finish line. It's hard to do things like that at the race track with so many people around. But then when I get them home, it's another thing. That's when I pet them and talk to them.

Huslia
Nov. 6 - 70

Dear Bella
If you know how much your dogs can take and in a race you got all you can from them even if you didn't do anything in the race you should be satisfied.

Be you next time

Sincerely
George

Any time a man can get everything his dogs have got, whether they won the race or came in 15th out of 20 teams, this man should be a happy man. I've come in as far back as seventh in a race and been satisfied because that was a seventh place team I had.

Dog racing isn't for a person who isn't satisfied when he gets the best out of his dogs.

THE BIG PLAN

I consider myself a professional musher. I don't go into a race just for the fun of it. I go in there to win. If I don't win, I want to be pressing the man who does win. I want to make him race to beat me. And while I'm doing this, I'm making money.

I plan my winter like a poker player. I look at the pots.

I got about 24 dogs that I carry with me. Out of this truckload of 24 dogs, there is just only so many good ones in there. Say maybe all I got is 14 top notch dogs. When I hit the Kenai race I cut out maybe four of the best dogs and save them for the Rendezvous. I race with 14 down in Kenai. I would like to win, but whether I do or not doesn't make that much difference. If I am pressing that front runner, that's the idea I go in there with. If my dogs weren't good enough to do this, I would know it, and I wouldn't be thinking this way.

In the preliminary races I just kind of split my top dogs up. At Kenai I leave some of them out. But in a big race like Rendezvous that really counts, I put my whole top string together. This is the first race of the year that these dogs run together. I don't put a big string like that together until I feel that this is it, this is the big one, and they are going to pay me back. If you put a whole batch of top notch dogs like that together, there has got to be some of them getting hurt. At least that is the way I look at it. When the pot isn't there, you just don't put everything in it.

If I am racing every weekend for say two months, and if I shoot for every race, that team has got to go sour somewhere along the line. There is no way I can keep that team at its peak every weekend. What I do is I shoot for the State Championship at Kenai, the Rendezvous, the North American, the Tok Race of Champions and the Tanana race. Those five races I shoot for. This year if I race outside I will be shooting for Ely and Kalkaska, too.

The State Championship and the Rendezvous are usually two weeks apart, so I got a chance to peak my dogs out for those two races. The Rendezvous and the North American are a month apart, so I got a chance to bring my dogs back up there. The Tok Race of Champions is the week after, and I could figure that all the top teams by then are just as tired as mine is. When I get up to the Tanana race the week after, the weather is usually a little bit cooler, and the dogs are pretty lively for that race.

After Rendezvous is Nenana. This is a smaller race. What I do is run 10 or 12 of my poorest dogs at Nenana and maybe get in some training. I don't put in any dog that I might hurt in this race, especially not my main leader. I leave him home. I enter that race knowing that even if I come in third or fourth, I am going to make expenses or maybe end up a little ahead.

Then by the North American in Fairbanks I got my team going again. Naturally I go in with the idea of winning that race. I run that race all out. Maybe I win and maybe I don't but I am going to come close. If I lose it, that is just the way the ball bounces. Maybe a few things that I didn't expect happened in there. Make just one little slip, maybe misjudge one dog, and the thing is lost. That is how close that race is.

A week later I go to Tok. Say I had one dog that was slightly stiff. I know he would help me for the two days of racing in Tok, but by then I am thinking of the Tanana race, too, so I drop him out. Maybe he is one of my best dogs, but if I am going to come out ahead dollar-wise at the end of the year, I got to gamble like this. I don't use this dog, knowing that if I lose this one, he will make it up for me the next week. So I go into this race with the best I could put together without hurting myself for Tanana. I go into the Tok race with the idea of winning it. It is the same thing over again. Maybe I do and maybe I don't, but actually I am doing the best I could do.

Next weekend when I get to Tanana, that is the last big race of the season. By this time a lot of my best dogs are lame and couldn't run no more. I go into that race with the best I can get out of my kennel. I go in with the idea of winning.

After Tanana my dogs have raced most every year in either Galena or Hughes. But some years I have quit after Tanana, knowing that I had already got too much out of my dogs. I didn't want to put them through another week of really hard running. It all depends on how the dogs look. You don't want to hurt the dogs. You don't want to hurt them in the mind. You can get just so much out of an animal before he says, "To heck with it. This is too much."

When you run your dogs to get everything out of them every race, naturally a dog can just take so much of that. It has got to give somewhere. Remembering that you want to keep running those dogs year after year, there is a point where you just have to quit. You could see when a dog has just about had it for the year. He starts acting up then. I've never had a team just lie down and quit on me, but I could see when they are on the edge of it. That is when I quit on a dog team. I tie them up and don't race them no more. Already by that time I am starting to plan for the next year.

I was saying back there in the beginning that there aren't as many dog teams as there used to be in the villages.

This isn't just because they use a lot of snow travelers now. The guys in the villages have dogs, but it is hard for them to compete with the teams from Fairbanks and Anchorage any more. A lot of times fellows come in to Fairbanks or Anchorage and finish far back because the competition today is much tougher speed-wise than it used to be. I don't think the dogs are any faster today than they were say 12 years ago. It is just the training and the feeding that is making them run faster. The teams that are winning up here in Alaska are moving as fast as any dog team can move and still make it for the 20 miles.

It is really tough up there today. Just a few years ago maybe a guy could win some of these races by 10 minutes. But you take the North American this past winter, 1971. The first team won by just a little better than a minute. (This is a 70 mile race. Ed.) And you could count half a dozen teams that were within a couple of minutes of each other. When you say you are five minutes behind, you sound good. But then when you say what place you finished, you don't sound so good any more. So maybe a guy does have an unusually good dog team. A lot of times we either win by the breaks, or we lose by the breaks. It works both ways. That is the reason a lot of guys are not coming out of the bush to race any more.

Another thing is that the expense is so high. The freight for one dog from Huslia to Anchorage is something like $25. And the airlines wouldn't furnish the crates for the dogs any more, so we have to buy the crates. A crate runs $20. I've managed to crowd four dogs into a crate, but maybe I've got 24 dogs, so it will take me six crates just to get my team here. So the expense is just too great for a lot of mushers back in the bush. There are good teams up there, but they can't get in to prove how good they are, so they can't get a sponsor.

Take Carl Huntington, for example. He started racing two years ago. He finished fifth in the Rendezvous in '70 and '71. You can't do it all in one year. He did have a sponsor this winter. I think they paid his way down and back and his entry fee. Actually it takes much more than that. You have to feed the dogs all year and do a lot of traveling around to the villages to get dogs to lease or buy. A lot of money is put down before you even enter a race. If I didn't have a good sponsor, there would be no way I could do it. No way I could meet all the expenses I have to go through before the race.

I believe that if some of these guys had good backing over a number of years, like my sponsors do for me, then we would get some new names in dog racing that would come up with good teams.

I was kinda busy this last month and a half or so in Anchorage. I was working for Jolly Electric Company. Where I did that last taping from was from my house. I am renting a house in Anchorage. Now I am working for the Yukon Transportation Company and am on the boat. You could hear the generators running maybe. We are tied up to the beach right now. This is a pretty good boat. It is a new one out of Juneau. We've got 23 people living aboard, and we have all sorts of things like a big living room, washer and dryer, showers, sink in every room and stuff like that. Actually I'm not doing much right now. These oil people only want to go about 20 miles a day, so I'm only working about three and a half hours, and that is it. (George is the pilot. Ed.) I don't have nothing to do the rest of the time, so I've been writing a lot of letters.

I am going to send these tapes off from Anvik. The mail service is really terrible here on the lower Yukon. I hope it gets better on the middle Yukon.

Well, if you got any more questions, just send them on.

See you guys. 'Bye.

APPENDIX

Crossing the finish line, 1972 Rendezvous, with a winning margin of eight minutes.   (photo by Maxine Vehlow)

"Grover did it for me." George with his lead dog after winning the 1972 Rendezvous in Anchorage.   (photo by Maxine Vehlow)

GEORGE ATTLA'S
1972
Sled Dog Racing Record

BEMIDJI, Minnesota: Jan. 8-9
 14 miles each day; 10 teams.
 1st Attla - 1 hr., 50 min., 50 secs.
 2nd Merve Hilpipre, Iowa - 1 hr., 55 min., 14 secs.

ELY, Minnesota: **All American Championship**, Jan. 15-16
 17 miles each day; 17 teams.
 1st Dick Moulton, New Hampshire - 2 hrs., 5 min., 7 secs.
 2nd Attla - 2 hrs., 7 min., 5 secs.

KALKASKA, Michigan: Jan. 29-30
 18 miles each day; 22 teams.
 1st Attla - 2 hrs., 3 min., 35 secs.
 2nd Moulton - 2 hrs., 3 min., 54 secs.

ANCHORAGE, Alaska, Fur Rendezvous: **World Championship**, March 17-19
 25 miles each day; 22 teams.
 1st Attla - 5 hrs., 15 min. 25 secs.
 2nd Gareth Wright, Fairbanks - 5 hrs., 23 min., 14 secs.

NENANA, Alaska: Feb. 26-27
 14 miles each day.
 1st Attla - 1 hr., 24 min., 50 secs.
 2nd Jerry Riley, Nenana - 1 hr., 26 min., 26 secs.

FAIRBANKS, Alaska: **North American Championship**, March 17-19
 20 miles 1st and 2nd days, 30 miles 3rd day; 17 teams.
 1st Attla - 4 hrs., 19 min., 33 secs.
 2nd Wright - 4 hrs., 25 min., 20 secs.

TOK, Alaska: **Race of Champions**, March 25-26
    20 miles each day; 11 teams.
    1st Attla - 2 hrs., 49 min., 47 secs.
    2nd Moulton - 2 hrs., 51 min., 51 secs.

TANANA, Alaska: **Yukon River Championship**, April 1-2
    16 miles each day; 10 teams.
    1st Attla - 1 hr., 58 min., 51 secs.
    2nd John Greenway, Fairbanks - 2 hrs., 6 min., 0 secs.

This record earned for George the **Gold Medal** in the International Sled Dog Racing Association's first annual competition for a **Point Champion**.

GLOSSARY

Alaskan Husky: A name applied to an Arctic-type crossbreed.
Attitude Run: A short outing under optimum conditions which the dogs thoroughly enjoy.
Athabascan Indians: Indians of a tribe living about Lake Athabasca, northern Alberta and Saskatchewan, Canada. (From Webster)
Athapascan: Pertaining to or designating an extensive linquistic family of North American Indians including the Athabascans, Navahos and Apaches. (From Webster)
Backline: Line from harness to towline. Same as tugline. (See diagram)
Basket: The part of the sled which holds the passenger or load. (See diagram)
Bridle: An arrangement of ropes and a ring attached permanently under the sled to which the towline is fastened.
Cache: A small log cabin on stilts used to store meat. It is built high enough off the ground to keep the meat out of reach of scavenging animals.

Cart Training: Training the dogs with a light, three or four wheeled vehicle.

Chain, Dog: A length of chain about five feet long with snaps on each end used to tether a dog.

Chief: With the Indians of Alaska the post is elective, like a mayor. A man who has held the post for many years retains the title after his retirement.

Depo-Medrol: Brand name for a pain-killing drug.

Dog Box: A large plywood box divided into individual compartments which is mounted on a truck and used to transport a dog team.

Dog Yard, Lot: The area at a musher's home where his dogs are kept.

Dragging: When a dog, either on or off his feet, is pulled along by his neckline.

Ely: A town in northern Minnesota which hosts one of the country's major races.

Fairbanks, Trail Leader: A leader which is good at stringing the team out but is not so good on commands. So named because the trail of the North American at Fairbanks has few places where a dog can get off.

Fishback Harness: X-back design harness originating in Fairbanks and made by Mrs. Mel Fishback, co-owner with her husband, Lee, of Zima Products, Nevada City, California 95959.

Hook, Snow Hook: A sharp piece of curved metal attached to the bridle of the sled by a line and used to hold the team either by being stomped into the snow or wrapped around a tree. (See diagram)

"Huslia Hustler": A title of honor which has been given to a succession of winning mushers from Huslia. In recent years it has been held by George Attla.

Indian Dog: An Arctic-type dog from an Indian village.

Jingler: About 10 bottle caps strung on a stiff wire loop. When grasped in the hand and shaken, the caps make a noise which attracts the dogs' attention.

Kalkaska: A town in northern Michigan which hosts one of the country's major races.

Kasco: Brand name of a dry dog food used by many mushers.
Lower 48 or 49: The states of the United States other than Alaska.
Mush!: From "marche," the familiar imperative form of the French verb *marcher,* to walk or march. A fictional command to start a dog team moving. *To mush dogs:* To drive a team.
Musher: From the French verb, *marcher,* to walk or march. The person who drives a dog team.
Neckline: Line from collar to towline. (See diagram)
Outside: Anywhere beyond the border of Alaska, usually the southern United States.
Overflow: Water on top of a frozen lake. This condition occurs when the weight of snow and ice in the middle of a lake causes the ice to sink a little. Then water escapes from around the shore and flows to the middle of the lake to equalize its level.
Pink Pads: A lack of pigment in the dog's pad.
Polyethylene: A plastic. Used here in the form of a braided rope. The rope comes in several thicknesses and several bright colors.
Potlatch: An Indian party characterized by an abundance of food and contests of various kinds.
Ptarmigan: Any of various species of grouse of northern regions having completely feathered feet. (From Webster) The Willow Ptarmigan is the Alaska state bird.
P-Tex: A yellow plastic commonly used on skis. It comes in strips 1/16" thick and cut as wide as the sled runner. It is usually glued to the bottom of the runner. It is both hard to glue on and easily scratched, so one run over a poorly covered trail can ruin a set of runners.
Pumping, Pedaling: Standing with one foot on one runner and pushing the sled with the other foot, like riding a scooter.
Punchy: A condition of the snow when the crust on top of soft snow becomes unable to support the weight of a dog.
Punching Through: When the dog's foot breaks through the crust of snow.
Rendezvous, Fur Rendezvous: From the French *rendez-vous,* an appointment. A week-long winter festival in Anchorage.

It started in 1936 as a series of sporting events without a name. In 1937 trappers gathered to join in the fun and also sell their furs. Thus the name used by the early French-Canadians, Indians and Mountain Men for their winter gathering to sell furs to traders was applied to this modern carnival. A fur auction is still held, along with many displays, contests and dances.

Dog racing began as a four team demonstration in 1946 and is now the most important event of the festival. Schools are closed on Friday, the first day of the race, as the whole city turns out to watch the teams.

Rondy: An Anglicized nickname for the Anchorage Fur Rendezvous.

Seppala, Leonhard: A Norwegian who lived in Nome circa 1915-1926. He was famous for his dog racing expertise, his participation in the bringing of diphtheria serum by dog team into Nome during the 1925 epidemic, and his own strain of Siberian Huskies.

The 1967 Iditarod Trail Centennial Race starting from Knik was declared a memorial to Leonhard Seppala, who had died only two weeks before it was held. Mrs. Constance Seppala drew the number one starting position which was retired in honor of her husband.

Sled Bag: A small bag, usually canvas, fastened inside the basket, in which are carried objects needed during the race.

Snow Berm: A ridge of snow. In this case made at the side of a road by a snow plow.

Snow Fence: Light weight fencing made of wooden uprights fastened together by wire.

Snow Traveler, Snowgo: Snowmobile.

Stanchions: The vertical parts of a sled. (See diagram)

Stove Up: Lame, stiff.

Swing Dogs: The dogs hitched into the team behind the leader. (See diagram)

Team Dogs: The dogs hitched into the team between the swing dogs and the wheel dogs. (See diagram)

Towline, Gangline: The center line fastened to the sled to which the dogs are hitched. (See diagram)

Tugline, Tug: Line from harness to towline. Same as backline. (See diagram)

Wheel Dogs, Wheelers: The dogs hitched nearest to the sled. (See diagram)

Wien: An airline which serves the interior of Alaska.

RACING SLED

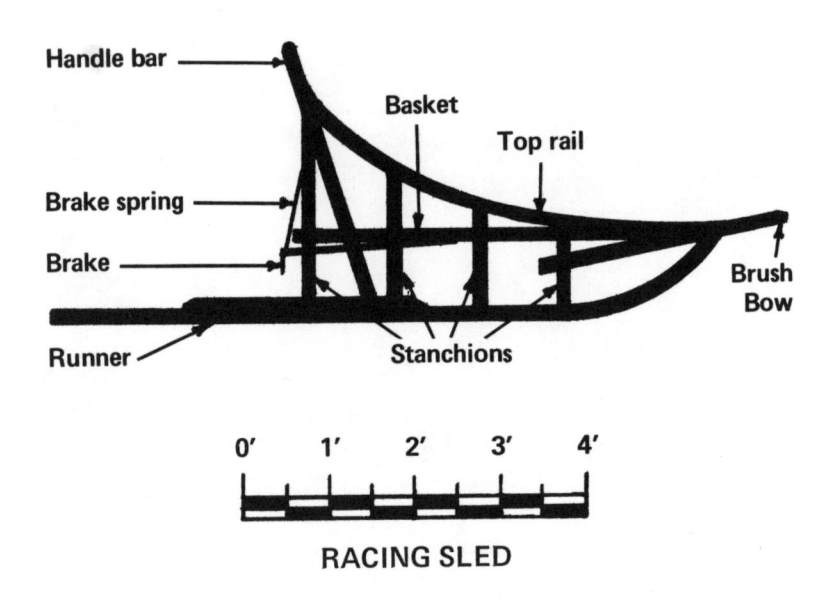

Labels: Handle bar, Basket, Top rail, Brake spring, Brake, Brush Bow, Runner, Stanchions

DOG TEAM

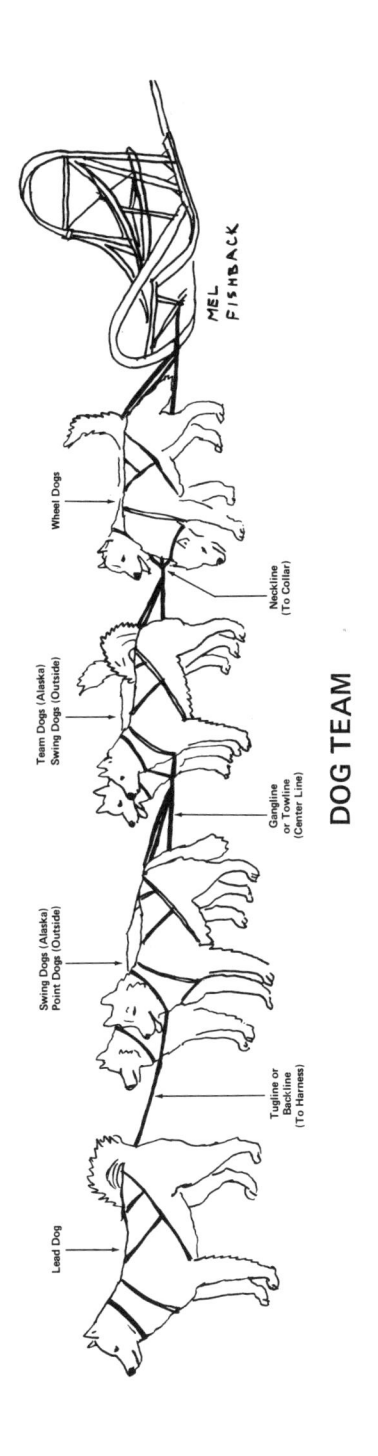

- Lead Dog
- Swing Dogs (Alaska) / Point Dogs (Outside)
- Team Dogs (Alaska) / Swing Dogs (Outside)
- Wheel Dogs
- Tugline or Backline (To Harness)
- Gangline or Towline (Center Line)
- Neckline (To Collar)

MEL FISHBACK

The IDITAROD
The Most Demanding Race of All

AS TOLD BY
GEORGE ATTLA

TO
BELLA LEVORSEN

I have included the following section of background information to make sure that the reader is familiar with the historical significance of this race. Ed.

Beyond Knik –

The IDITAROD Trail !

There were riches beyond that long ago anchorage on Upper Cook Inlet. There was wealth in gold and furs in Alaska's interior. And there were hardy souls who toiled to bring it out. Even to those early pioneers the Iditarod Trail was legend. It was their lifeline to the world Outside.

Development of the Iditarod Trail began a number of years before the Iditarod gold finds. Since 1898 the boom town of Knik had served as a freighting center in central Alaska. Trails from Knik established by the Alaska Road Commission wound from one gold field to another between Seward and Nome.

On Christmas day, 1908 two prospectors, John Beaton and Harry Dychman, struck it rich and triggered activity in Iditarod which by 1910 boosted the population of the region to 2,500 miners, storekeepers, cooks and the like.

A 1914 mining journal recorded, "During the winter, transportation is effected mainly by dog teams, or, on well-beaten trails, by horse-drawn sleds. Roadhouses are maintained at intervals along the main lines of travel and afford food and shelter for both persons and animals. The main winter trail from Iditarod to the sea . . . . . runs in general east-west to McGrath, thence up the Kuskokwim River across the divide at Rainy pass, thence southeastward . . . . . to Knik, a distance of about 500 miles.

" . . . . . Other much traveled trails lead from Iditarod to the Yukon and Tanana. Many of the trails are staked and flagged by the Alaska Road Commission, so that they are recognizable even in severe storms, which are by no means infrequent."

The importance of this trail was not restricted to miners and their supplies. In 1908 the United States government let a contract to transport mail over the winter months. From Knik dog teams, varying in size from 7 to 12 dogs, mushed into the winter storms with mail destined for delivery in Nome and all points in between.

(The above information was taken from an article by Dick Wolff, *Anchorage Daily News,* December 4, 1966.)

At the end of January, 1925 when the diptheria epidemic struck Nome, this same system of native mail team dog drivers was alerted from Nenana to Unalakleet by telephone. As soon as the serum from Anchorage arrived at the end of the railroad line in Nenana (see map inside front cover), native teams took it over and passed it from roadhouse to roadhouse where fresh teams were waiting. Day and night 12 teams of Indians and Eskimos plus 5 teams of white men carried the 20 pound package of serum through some of the worst weather on record all the way to the coast and beyond Shaktoolik. There it was passed on to Leonhard Seppala who took it to Golovin. Charlie Olson took it to Bluff, and Gunnar Kaasan brought it the last 53 miles into Nome. As the serum progressed along the trail from Galena to Nulato to Kaltag to Old Woman to Unalakleet, no thought of money or glory entered the drivers' minds. They were unhesitantingly laying their lives and the lives of their dogs on the line to help their fellow man, as was Alaskan custom at the time. (From conversations with Jimmy and

"Map courtesy of British Petroleum, Alaska."

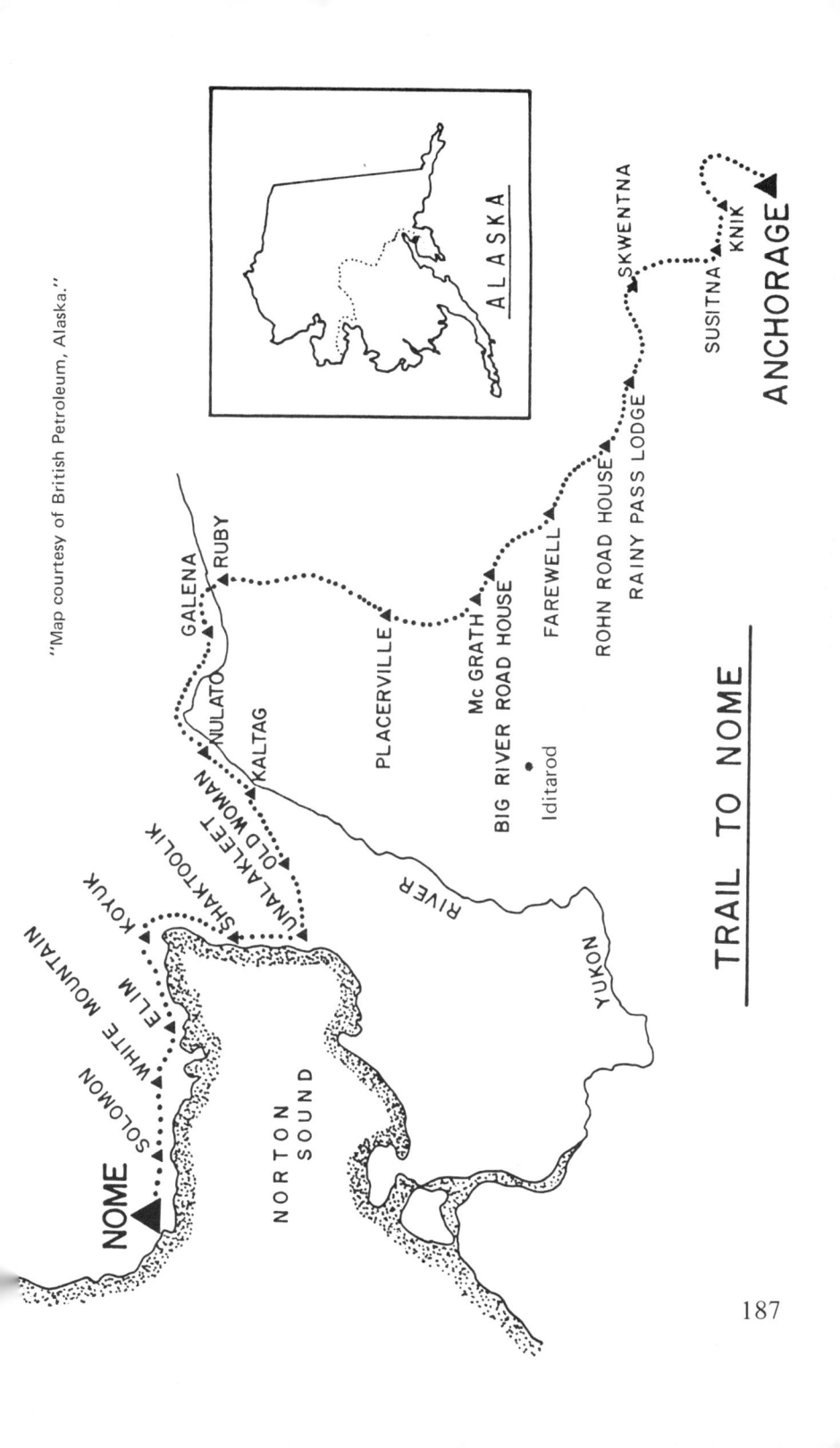

ALASKA

TRAIL TO NOME

Sidney Huntington of Galena; Charlie Evans and Edgar Nollner, also of Galena who were drivers in the run; Ella Vernetti of Koyukuk, who with her husband ran the trading post in Koyukuk when the serum came through. Recorded in Galena and Koyukuk November, 1973 by Oren Johnson of Anchorage. And from an article by Sasha Kahanaha, *Anchorage Daily News,* February 4, 1970. Ed.)

Little remains today of either Knik or Iditarod. But Joe Redington, Sr., who had a homestead on the trail outside of Knik, had dreamed for years of having a sled dog race along the historic trail. In 1967 Joe and his Iditarod Trail Committee had put on a race over a short portion of the trail from Knik to Big Lake. Now he planned a race all the way from Anchorage to Nome. Joe and the committee hoped that if the trail were opened up again and the old roadhouses restored, eventually the government would take over the system and preserve it as part of our heritage.

Putting on the race was a monumental job. The Iditarod Trail Committee enlisted the aid of the U.S. Army which sent out parties during the summer to find the old trail and the roadhouses. A week before the race the Army sent crews and machines - - officially on winter maneuvers - - to break the trail and mark it for the racers. The Air Force supplied the services of its veterinarian, Captain Terry Adkins, who traveled the entire length of the trail throughout the race to check dogs.

The Iditarod Trail Committee organized the voluntary aid of hundreds of private and commercial airplane pilots, snowmobilers, ham radio operators, and people living along the trail. Nome's Mayor Robert Renshaw said, "No single event has generated as much excitement here since the days of the Gold Rush."

Then the committee went into debt to finish raising the promised $50,000 prize money.

The rules of the race were based on those of the old All Alaska Sweepstakes, a sled dog race held annually between 1908 - 1916 from Nome to Candle and return, a total distance of 408 miles. The racers traveled and camped at their own speed. They had to carry certain survival equipment. They were required to stop at all checkpoints, established about 50 miles apart, where every dog had to be accounted for. Dogs not able to continue could be dropped off at these checkpoints. One racer who dropped a dog at what he thought was an official checkpoint had to go back for him to avoid disqualification. Dropped dogs were flown by the committee either back to Knik or on to the finish.

On March 3, 1973, 34 teams left Anchorage; 22 of them made it 1,169 miles to Nome.

George Attla was in the race. Here is his account.

The Great Camping Trip

GETTING READY

October - November

The first thing I am going to do is to fill you in on how I got ready for the race. How I picked my dogs out.

When I started training my dogs last year, what I was looking for was the usual speed dogs. I was trying to put a team together for the Anchorage Rendezvous and the Fairbanks North American. I guess you know I lost some of those dogs I had the year before; two leaders, Grover and Swift, and then I lost three other team dogs. When I started training I worked with Mac McLean's whole team, so I had a lot of dogs to work with, but they weren't anything to compare to the year before.

I wasn't thinking much about the Iditarod then. I wasn't too sure it was going to come off. But I had it in the back of my mind. So what I did was put together the best team I could for the Anchorage and Fairbanks races, and I just figured that whatever I have left over that can't make the main team I'd start training for the Iditarod. And that's the way I worked it.

I picked up some dogs from around Fairbanks too, ones that other mushers said weren't fast enough for their teams but that they thought would do me good in the Iditarod. So I had 13 dogs that I started training for the Iditarod, and there wasn't a dog in there that could make the Anchorage race with my other team.

December - January 25

For this long race all I wanted was fast trotters; dogs that didn't have to run, just trot fast. So I hooked all 13 of them up at one time, and then with my regular race sled I just drug a tire behind the sled. Sometimes I used two tires if it was too rough. What I tried to do was to make them trot as fast as they could, just steadily.

These were good dogs, you know. They were just a notch under what you would run in the Rendezvous, so really they were trying to run. Some of these dogs I had worked on already, say for a month and a half, trying to bring them along to where they would make it for the shorter races. But I found they couldn't cut it. When a dog can't cut it, then usually his spirit will break down. He loses all his life, all his eagerness.

I found that when I cut these dogs back and started just trotting instead of running, then after a couple of weeks of wanting to run but not letting them, they were really eager to go. They got all their life back and everything.

I was training them maybe 10 mile runs and 25 mile runs. I never went no further than 25 miles. Not one run before I got into the Iditarod. And all the time I kept them just under a lope, almost running, but just trotting.

When I first started these dogs they really couldn't trot, but after roughly a month and a half of working with them, of making trotters out of them, they could do a pretty good job. And they were lively. There was no force on them anywhere. They could do 25 miles with no problem at all, just trotting as fast as they can. I mean they could really move out. On a good hard trail with a tire behind them they were clipping off easily 12 miles an hour.

Just the same way you build up a dog's loping speed, you can build up his trotting speed too. At least this is what I figured. You know I have never done it before, but I figured it has got to come out that way. And it did come out that way.

January 25

I had 35 dogs or so in the yard that I was working. I had my race team for the Rendezvous; you know, three different teams that I was running about 15 miles a day each team. And then I was running this Iditarod team 25 miles a day. And about three weeks before the Rendezvous I found that I just couldn't do it. I was covering too many miles a day. The day just wasn't long enough. So I got Winkler Bifelt from Huslia to come and help me. Then he started running the Iditarod team 25 miles a day.

When I went out to make the race circuit, I left Winkler with the Iditarod dogs and told him what I wanted: 25 miles a day, roughly five days out of the week.

February 3 - 25

Karen and I were gone about three weeks to the Anchorage race (February 16, 17, 18) and then to the Kenai race (February 24, 25). The Iditarod was going to be the week after the Kenai.

I really hadn't made up my mind to get in this Iditarod race. I figured I'd let Winkler do it, although I never did really say that this is what I am going to do.

Actually before Winkler came to help, I approached my brother Alfred and asked him if he wanted to run in the Iditarod race. If he wanted to, I would have a team for him.

He was in Fairbanks and over to the house when I asked him if he would do it. And he said, "I'll let you know when I get home." He is living in Hughes now, and he said, "I'll ask my wife and see if it's okay with her, and if it's okay with her, I'll run the race."

So he went back up to Hughes and about three or four days later he called me up and said that he wouldn't be able to do it. (Alfred is shown in the foreground of the bottom picture, page 153. A younger brother, Barney, is in the background. Ed.)

So actually a week before the race I hadn't made up my mind yet. I was wanting to race in the Fairbanks North American, which was the same time as the Iditarod; but in Anchorage I came in fourth, and that was a big struggle just to come in fourth. Then I had a couple of bad runs in Kenai. I was putting a lot of new dogs together and trying to make a race, and I just couldn't do it.

Bud Smyth would have lent me his best race dogs to enter the North American, but even with them I still wouldn't have had enough good dogs, a good enough team to win the race in Fairbanks. It looked like a losing battle to me. So after the Kenai race I made up my mind. I thought, "Well, I'll just get in on this great big camping trip."

February 26, 27

Karen and I went back to Fairbanks. I dumped my race dogs and we picked up 12 of the Iditarod team dogs. I put four of my race dogs in there, too. I picked the race dogs that weren't really too hard workers, ones that would just pace themselves. The ones that work too hard for a race like that I gave to Mac McLean for his team for the North American.

Of the race dogs I took Little Toughie, who is with the pictures of the three well-built dogs. And Tootsie who is in the book. And Kasin who was on the '72 team too. Kasin is litter mate to Scotty. These three dogs all ran in the Rendezvous race this year. (They are shown on the back cover of the book. The front dogs in that picture, reading from left to right are: Grover, Swift, Tex, Jarvi, Scotty, Tootsie, Kasin, Little Toughie. Ed.) And then I had Sparky, a Norris dog, that I had raced at Kenai. She was another good race dog.

The race dogs weren't trained for this, but I figured that they were good enough to be able to take going on a long trotting trip. I figured it would be a regular camping trip. There is no way you are going to turn a 1,000 mile race into a racing thing. You can't put pressure on the dogs. They got to do it on their own. I figured that as long as a dog is tough, he could take going a long distance at a trotting speed. And it pretty much worked out that way.

February 28 - March 2

So Karen and Winkler and I headed for Anchorage. Then we started rushing around getting ready. This was roughly three days before the race. It took the whole family. Like Lawrie and Virginia Gay were running all over town picking up stuff for me. (Lawrie Gay, a dog musher in his own right, is manager of British Petroleum, Alaska, which is now sponsoring George. Ed.)

My mother was in Anchorage and she was sewing new soles on my boots. I had native made boots, wolf leg boots with moose hide bottoms. Then I had canvas leg boots with moose hide bottoms. I had three pairs. You know I wore those boots the whole trip and I never wore through any of them. But my feet got pretty sore the last 200 miles.

I had a lot of extra sox, too, two changes besides what I had on my feet. And I had an extra set of clothes. All this gear was in case I got wet.

When I started I had enough food for myself to last as far as Ruby, or I thought it would get me to Ruby. The way it wound up, as slow as I was going, it didn't last that long. What we did for food was we put a bunch of sliced-up potatoes in with a steak and wrapped it in tinfoil. All I did was throw the tinfoil in the fire, and in roughly 15 minutes I had steak and fried potatoes. Everything was wrapped and ready to go, no extra gear or nothing.

I had about 200 pounds of gear on the sled to start with, and then at the end I don't think I had 50 pounds.

For the sled, my brother Robert, who lives in Anchorage, had been building it for me all along. I needed a different type of sled and so he made me a seven-foot basket sled. The sled wasn't finished until the morning of the Iditarod. Winkler and Robert had worked on it all that night. That is how late we were in getting ready.

On the picture of the sled and the dog pans that you wanted, (each dog pan was the bottom half of a large tin can with a wire handle attached. Ed.) well, I don't have the sled anymore. I had an accident out on the trail the other day. You would never believe it. I had 10 dogs and they hung me up on a fence. I didn't get hurt, but all they left was the back end of the sled. Me and my good leaders!

March 2

When we went to the drawing down there with the rest of the mushers for the Iditarod race, this was a new crowd altogether. Like 35 mushers in the bunch and the only people I knew in there were Bobby Vent - - he's from Huslia, you know - - and Issac Okleasik and Bud Smyth and Dick Mackey and Rayme Redington. The rest of the guys were all new faces. I didn't know who was who. I still haven't met some of the guys. I didn't know them when we started, and I never got to meet them on the trail. Then we came home before they got into Nome. Maybe I'll meet them sometime.

But I tell you, some of the other guys, I got to know them pretty good before the whole thing was over.

George with his wife Karen harnessing up the dogs. "Karen is the best dog handler I know." Robert Attla holds pair of dogs in front. Photograph by Charles Towill, Public Relations Manager of British Petroleum, Alaska. Courtesy of B.P. Alaska.

THE RACE

March 3 - Anchorage to Knik

When we started in Anchorage I had 16 dogs with Blue and Jarvi in lead. I had drawn number seven. Well, by the first 12 miles, by Eagle River, I had passed everybody in front of me, just trotting. I never did let the dogs run.

From Eagle River on I couldn't stay on the trail. That area is populated and there is no specific trail. There are roads all over and snowgo trails all over, and really it wasn't marked good enough. (Souvenir collectors had removed many markers. Ed.) Half the time I was lost. I must have gone 20 extra miles that day.

To give you an idea, Issac Okleasik, he started number 13 and that day I passed him six times. The last time I passed him was right at Knik River bridge, and then I left him again after that. During all this time when I was getting lost and stuff, I tore my brake off. I didn't have control of the dogs, and I crippled, heck, five dogs that first day. Three or four miles after Knik River bridge I had to load one of the dogs. Then another one was on the neckline before I got into Knik, and I had to load him, too, before I crossed the finish line. Issac and Herbert caught me just as I was coming into Knik. (To make a race within a race, the Iditarod Trail Committee awarded an extra $1,000 in gold nuggets to the first musher across the line in Knik. The 'gold poke' was won by Herbert Nayukpuk. Ed.)

Lawrie Gay, Manager of British Petroleum, Alaska, George's sponsor, holds lead dogs Jarvi and Blue while talking with Joe Redington, Sr. Robert Attla inspects the lines while Karen Attla brings up another dog.
Photo by Mike McDermott

At the 30 second countdown. The trail to Nome started at the Alaskan Sled Dog And Racing Association's permanent facility on Tudor Road, Anchorage.
Photo by Henry Peck

The start. George's mother watches.
Photograph by Charles Towill, Public Relations manager for British Petroleum, Alaska. Courtesy of B.P. Alaska.

Somewhere between Anchorage and Knik. "There was stretches where there was no snow at all." Robert Attla is running alongside the team. Winkler Bifelt is running to the left off the pavement.
Photo by Henry Peck.

So really I had a tough day. From Anchorage to Knik was probably the hardest part of the trail on the dogs' feet. There was stretches where there was no snow at all. And what snow we had was froze and crusted. A lot of us did lose dogs just because of bad feet in that area. I mean really bad going. Sparky, the Norris dog, went lame. Kasin went lame the first day, too, and she had never gone lame before.

I sort of ripped my team apart, which was pretty bad when you got 1,000 miles to go and you knock out five dogs the first day. So I dropped only three of the dogs and tried to go on with the rest.

I stayed overnight there in Knik. Some of the guys went on. Like Bobby Vent went roughly ten miles. Issac and Johnny Coffin and John Komack went five miles. Herbert Nayukpuk left Knik three times that night. You know, it was dark and he was getting lost and coming back into Knik. After the third time he gave it up and camped there in Knik.

"And what snow we had was froze and crusted." Winkler Bifelt watches the team leave the road. Photo by Henry Peck

March 4 - Knik to beyond Skwentna

The next morning I left at I think it was five o'clock. One team took off ahead of me. You know, I could hear them hooking up dogs. I didn't know who it was, but later on the trail I found out it was Seavey. Anyway, Issac and Komack and Johnny Coffin were in their camp when I came to them. They were just getting ready to leave so I stopped and had a cup of coffee and changed my boots.

When I caught Seavey up and passed him, my dogs just walked away from him. One team was just trotting faster than the other, two different sets of trotting.

As soon as I left Seavey I could see by the tracks that there was one more team ahead of me and I didn't know who it was. It must have been about 40 miles out of Knik that I caught Bobby. He kept up with me for a while, and then I left him. And all of this was just trotting. My dogs weren't running or anything.

But what I did all the way on this race, like I'd be riding most of the time, but any time there was a hill, whether it was 100 feet long or a mile, I'd get off the sled and run the whole thing trying to keep drag off the dogs.

Anytime I got running up a hill I would be taking off extra gear so that I won't be sweating. You never want to work up a sweat so much that you are soaked and can't dry up. If you did this on a hill, once you get on flat going and start cooling off again, then if your clothes are wet it wouldn't be very hard to freeze.

It's 83 miles from Knik to Skwentna. It's a good stretch in there. There's no real hills and no water.

Anyhow, that second night I camped about seven miles past Skwentna. It was seven o'clock and getting dark already. When I was putting up camp Bobby Vent caught up with me, and he camped with me.

I don't remember how cold it was that night, but it was cold. But I had good gear. One thing a musher has got to have when he is going to something like this is a good sleeping bag and plenty of food. I think a good sleeping bag is the main thing. I had a down sleeping bag and then I had a blanket inside too. There wasn't a night I was cold.

Another thing I have learned on all the camping trips I have taken is that you can't keep warm if you sleep with your sox and stuff on. Even if your sox are damp at the end of the day, if you take them off and leave them in your sleeping bag with you, they will dry up from your body heat there in the night. But if you leave them on, then the dampness will stay in there and you don't have a chance of keeping warm the next day if it is cold again.

When I make camp I put spruce boughs under the dogs and I put spruce boughs under my sleeping bag. It is a lot of work. Say I am ready to go to bed roughly three hours after I stop.

Somewhere near Skwentna George turns to watch the plane from which this picture was shot.
Photograph by Charles Towill, Public Relations Manager for British Petroleum, Alaska. Courtesey of B.P. Alaska.

March 5 - Skwentna to Rainy Pass Lodge

The next morning Bobby took off first and I caught him up in about two miles. During the night somebody had passed us. I found out it was Johnny Coffin from Noorvik when we passed him while he was still making breakfast. Bobby must have kept up with me for seven or eight miles that morning, and then I never saw him again.

That was really a rough day. Remember I said I crippled five dogs that first day and left three of them in Knik? Well, that day I had to drop the other two off at a checkpoint.

There was a lot of hills and a lot of running that day. The trail was really crooked in there. The Army was breaking the trail and they had snowgos that could back up. Places that was really brushy, they would go ahead a little bit and back up, and that was the only way they could make some of the turns. When we came along, we had to do a lot of running just to get around those turns.

And then, you know, we didn't come straight down off the hills. We would zig-zag around trees. Some of those hills in there that we had to come off of were really bad. I wouldn't have come off some of them with those turns if I had known what I was getting into. We had a hard time making them with a dog team.

Anyway, that day I camped about five or six miles before I got to Rainy Pass Lodge, and I got there about three o'clock in the afternoon. If I had known I was that close to the lodge, I would have kept going.

I knew I was in the lead then. From what I'd seen my dogs do with their trotting speed and nobody catching me up, I thought, "Well, these dogs can trot as fast or faster than any team in the race." So that was the reason I camped early that day.

I found on this trip that if you could get up at three in the morning and take off at five, then you can stop at three in the afternoon or so and make a good camp. It's better to travel early and stop early while it is still daylight and you can see what you are doing. Then you could get all kinds of wood for in the morning, and you could bed your dogs down good. In the interior we had a lot of trees, and I took the harnesses off and tied the dogs to trees. Then I always put spruce boughs under the dogs to give them a chance to dry off in the night and so they are not laying in the snow.

The first part of this race the dogs could travel only so many hours a day before they got tired. I'd say 12 hours was all they could take. So I traveled early and made camp early. Towards the end it didn't matter so much. The dogs could go a lot longer, and there are no trees for spruce boughs or firewood on the coast. So it really didn't matter if you were traveling in the daytime or in the dark. When you travel in the dark you can't see nothing, but your dogs could feel the trail. They know when they get off the trail.

About seven that evening Johnny Coffin came and camped with me. After that I was asleep and didn't know whether anybody passed me or not.

Musher John Schulz maneuvering his sled through Ptarmigan Pass. Photo by musher Casey Celusnick of Cee-Jae Kennels' "Gen-U-Wine Alaskan Fishburners."

March 6 - Rainy Pass Lodge to Rohn Roadhouse

The next morning I got up first and left before Johnny did. I think the most determined man I saw in the whole race was Johnny Coffin; you know, determined to make it there.

Rainy Pass Lodge was five or six miles, and when I got there people were just getting up. I came in and they offered me breakfast. I found out that Dick Wilmarth had passed me during the night. I didn't know who Dick Wilmarth was, but I met him that morning. He said he got there about one o'clock in the morning.

I had a dog food cache there at Rainy Pass Lodge so I took on some more dog food. My dogs had the runs by then from overfeeding commercial dog food. I could see that they were losing weight, but I was stuck with what I had. You know, I was in the middle of nowhere by then.

I made a good run that day. It was good moving all the way through Rainy Pass. Actually we didn't go by way of Rainy Pass, we went through Ptarmigan Pass. (The snow-mobiles couldn't get through Rainy Pass. Ed.) Coming through Ptarmigan Pass up to Rohn River was some of the most beautiful scenery I've seen yet. On a trip like this you see moose, and I saw caribou coming through the pass. The weather was beautiful, and the scenery was just, you know, beautiful.

Then starting roughly 20 miles above Rohn River and coming down Rohn River, it was nothing but glare ice and gravel. I had plastic on the bottom of my runners about ¼ of an inch thick. I found that this plastic would run just about as easy on gravel as it would on snow. Iron would usually grab on rocks, but this was a completely different thing. So actually it wasn't too bad, except there is no way you could stop your dogs on glare ice, and there was a lot of open water in that area too.

I really didn't know my way. There was supposed to be some civilian snow travelers ahead of the first musher, but then I caught them at Finger Lake the day before and they were still there when I left. I had maps and knew there was supposed to be a cabin somewhere so I started hunting around. I found the cabin, and there was a young couple there. So I got to Rohn Roadhouse about seven o'clock.

I fed and watered the dogs. I'd always melt snow for water for the dogs to drink if there wasn't any. And I mixed their feed with water too. For dog food all I had was some commercial food and some dried fish. I should have got my dogs used to eating the dried fish before I left, but I just picked it up for the trip. Tallow is another thing I had. I would feed them a little bit of fish during lunch. This was at first. By the end of the trip I found out that on a long trip like this it took roughly three to four times the amount of food over what a dog normally eats during hard training.

At the end I was feeding those dogs roughly four meals a day; one big meal in the evening and a little piece of raw meat every time I stopped. I wasn't doing this to start with and they weren't getting enough feed, but then I didn't know this. It didn't come to me for a couple of days. I knew it was going to take more feed so I was giving them more food, but I was giving them more commercial food. After a couple of days the stuff started running right through them.

Anyhow, that evening only the snow travelers caught up. Nobody else got there. They all fell short of Rohn Roadhouse.

"In this area we were on the river and there was nothing but glare ice and sand and gravel." John Schulz and Casey Celusnick's team shown on the South Fork of the Kuskokwim River between Rohn Roadhouse and Farewell Lake. Photos by Casey Celusnick.

March 7 - Rohn Roadhouse through Farewell Lake Lodge

I left the next morning before the snowgos did, but five or six miles down below they caught me. In this area we were on the river and there was nothing but glare ice and sand and gravel. There was a lot of overflow and a lot of open water too. The open water was really bad. You couldn't tell the difference between water and ice because it all looked the same; the ice that was wind-blown and the water.

It is 40 miles going down the river to Farewell Lake Lodge. We had a tail wind, and sometimes my sled would be right up with the dogs. The dogs really had a hard time. They couldn't keep their footing on that stuff. Before we got to Farewell I was pretty well disgusted with the way conditions were.

The snowgos were having problems too. They were always getting stuck in the water and stuff. Sometimes they were ahead of me and sometimes I was ahead of them.

One place I just cut off the river altogether. I figured I was going to make a short cut through the woods. But I got back there and I had a heck of a time with no trail. The dogs were just going through the woods blind, and I was getting tangled up in brush and stuff like that. So I came back to the river again, and I was not too far behind the snowgos. I could see the signs.

When we got to Farewell Lake Lodge it must have been roughly noon. We stayed and had lunch. The guys with the snowgos took off and said they were going down to McGrath, and I figured I would just go down a little ways and camp. So I went roughly another 20, 25 miles. It was about 4, 5 o'clock in the afternoon.

Before I camped I noticed a plane was circling me. It was some travelogue photographer from out of state. (Art Hall from California filming Nicol Smith's "Alaska". Ed.) Only I didn't know this. He told me this when I got to McGrath. There was a lake not too far from the spot where I camped, and he said that they had landed there and waited for me so he could get some pictures, but I didn't show up. I just came to a good spot to camp, so I camped.

The report I got from Farewell was that the other guys were way back there yet. That is another reason I camped early. I figured, "Well, I'll just take my time."

Anyway, it was a good camp that evening. When I'm traveling like this I'd rather be alone. Then I could travel at my own speed, just do the things I want. It's easier for me then. I was enjoying myself just being out driving dogs and no rush.

Actually this Iditarod race is not a race at all. There is no way you are going to race 1,000 miles. You are just traveling. If you pushed your dogs they couldn't make 1,000 miles. They got to do it on their own. Now I've seen guys pop a whip behind their dogs out there on this Iditarod trail. If I did that to my dogs they couldn't have made the race because they are trained to listen to the whip. These guys that did it, the only reason I could see that their dogs made it was because they didn't respond to the whip.

March 8 - Into McGrath

I must have got up at one o'clock in the morning and was ready to go again. I don't know how many miles I covered before it got daylight, but you could travel pretty good in the dark because there was only one trail. Later that day we had to go through a lot of flats where the trail was wind-blown.

By this time I hadn't seen another musher for two days.

I don't really know how many miles I covered that day, but I drove a long ways. I must have got into McGrath about nine o'clock in the evening, and the dogs were really tired. Jarvi had sore feet and they kept getting worse and worse. Before we got to McGrath he was really bad off and I had him in the sled.

I knew by then that this commercial food I was feeding them wasn't staying with them. Running right through them.

That evening I ran into a guy that I went to school at Edgecumbe with and we were talking and he asked me what I was feeding my dogs. His name was Pete Mulluck. I told him I was feeding commercial food. And he said, "Why Jesus Christ, you know damn well you couldn't work on corn flakes. Do you expect your dogs to work on corn flakes? Go get some meat."

March 9 - In McGrath

So the next day I picked up a bunch of beaver meat there. And when I started feeding my dogs the beaver meat, I didn't know it at the time, but I still wasn't feeding them enough to hold them up in that kind of conditions.

I knew my dogs were tired and run down and losing weight pretty fast, so I laid over in there.

It took me six days to get into McGrath. The Army left Knik five days before I did and I got into McGrath two days behind them. I had gained three days on them. When I got to McGrath their trail was still good, and if I had kept going that next day, I would still have had the Army trail. The rules were that the civilian snowgos stick with the lead team. So if I had taken off with the civilian snowgos ahead of me, I would have had an open trail for the next couple of days anyhow.

But then that second night was when the storm came and the trail was blown over. You know we had a snowstorm starting from McGrath for three or four days when most of the time the planes weren't flying. If I had kept going that next day with the snowgos in front of me, that storm would have stopped everybody. The trail would have been closed off behind me.

But then I laid over in there with the idea of resting up my dogs. I didn't stay because of the storm, it was the condition of the dogs. I figured I couldn't get along without Jarvi. I knew I was going to have to haul him, so I figured that if I wait a day and then haul him on and off it would be okay. I figured I'd give all the dogs a day's rest and get the day back easy at the end.

But it didn't work out that way. That rest I gave my dogs there didn't really do them any good. I found out when I took off that they were still pretty much run down.

The first guy that came into McGrath behind me was Dick Wilmarth, and he was roughly 24 hours behind. I think there was something like nine teams that caught up in McGrath.

March 10 - McGrath to Bob's Cabin

I was the first one out of McGrath that second morning. I told the snow machine guys who were having breakfast that I was ready to go. This was roughly 5:30 in the morning.

It was snowing when we left, and it was pretty tough going all day. That night when I camped Seavey caught up with me.

We stayed in a guy's cabin. His first name was Bob, but, God dang it, I couldn't remember his last name. He works for F.A.A. in McGrath and he has a cabin roughly 60 miles out of McGrath. You know he just flew over there in that storm for the weekend. He told us he was going to be there before he left. He and his wife flew up the day we were leaving McGrath and built a fire in their cabin. When we got there the house was nice and warm and all kinds of food cooked, big turkey and all. I think his wife stayed there and did that for others as well. They must have put up a lot of mushers.

March 11 - Bob's Cabin to Bear Creek

Wilmarth had passed us during the night while we were sleeping, but I didn't know this until the next morning when I passed him while he was still in his camp. That day, while I was making lunch, Seavey caught me up. His dogs looked good to me and I knew mine were running down.

I left Seavey where we had lunch and then I met the civilian snowgos that were breaking trail for us. They were coming back. They said that the trail had turned off and that they had missed it and they thought they knew where they had lost it at. So I turned my dogs around and started to follow them. When we found the trail again we left a sign there at the turn saying that there was a cabin down there half a mile, but it was the wrong way to go unless you wanted to camp in that cabin.

So we kept going, and we had a hard time that day. We kept losing the trail. The trail the Army had broke was completely covered over.

These guys that were breaking trail on their snowgos were really a helpful bunch of guys, and they weren't going to get any prize money if they made it to Nome, either.

"... the dogs were really tired." Photographer unknown.

There was Bob Stone and Bill Copeland, and gosh dang, I don't remember the names of the others. I wish I did because a lot of this trail, especially between McGrath and Ruby, I don't think we could have made it without them. (An article in the *Anchorage Daily News* by Pam Randles says that the others were Joe Smith, Don Rosevear and Carl Fritzler. Ed.)

Anyway, that second day out from McGrath we were lost and wandering around there pretty much.

You know the Army was marking the trail with ribbons. What they did was just throw the ribbons on the snow where there was no stick to tie the ribbons onto. So we'd come to a great big flat after their trail was completely blown in, and you couldn't see the ribbons under the snow. Where there was trees and stuff they had all kinds of ribbons tied onto the trees; but through the flats where you really needed the ribbons, there was nothing to go by.

We were planning on camping in Bear Creek that night. Anyway, about seven miles out of Bear Creek we found our way again. It was all through the woods again. In here we came to this steep hill. We had a lot of hills, but this was a really steep climb. So I put on my snowshoes and walked up the hill behind my dogs. And I was thinking, "Well, hell, some of these guys will really have a hard time getting up this hill." That evening in Bear Creek when Seavey and Wilmarth caught up, I asked them if they had to walk up that hill. And they said, "No, we had no problem getting up there." That was when I found out just how much better shape their dogs were in than mine.

By that time I was pretty well out of feed too. I had enough for one more night. They had a radio there at Bear Creek, so I asked them to call into McGrath and say I needed some dog food. So they did that evening, but I didn't know who was going to bring it.

You know we all shipped our own dog food, at least I did, out to these checkpoints. The Iditarod Committee did have dog food caches along the trail in case anybody didn't have any. They were supposed to put in a cache at Bear Creek, but the cache wasn't there. (Weather prevented delivery, Ed.) For the civilian snow travelers there was no gas or nothing for them to go on with.

Tex Gates, the guy that owned the mining camp there, gave those guys gas and oil for their snowgos. That is the way they kept going. And they put us mushers up in a cabin and gave us food too. Some more nice people.

March 12 - Bear Creek to Somewhere North

The next day I left first again. You know I am not the kind of guy that can sit one place when I have some place to go.

My dogs were getting weaker all the time.

Anyhow, I was going through some flats and I saw this plane land ahead of me. But they took off before I got there. So I came to this big pile of fish they had dropped on the trail. I looked at it and couldn't tell whose name was on it. I didn't think it was for me so I didn't pick it up. I figured somebody else behind had ordered this feed. That night was the last feed I had for the dogs. I found out later that this fish was dropped off for me. To this day yet, I don't know who the pilot was who dropped this fish off.

The trail was really crooked that day. There was a lot of places we'd be following the trail the Army made and we'd make a circle and cross our own track almost. Like about five miles past Bear Creek we went down this one valley roughly 10 miles. I guess the Army went down this valley to the end and found out they were going the wrong way so they turned around and came back. And their trails ran about a half mile apart. We went down 10 miles one way and came back right alongside our own trail. Twenty miles of work and we made about a half mile of distance. It was really kind of disgusting, but you know, it was funny in a way too. You'd be going along and you know how far you got to go, and pretty soon you're crossing your own track.

That day I don't really know how many miles we went before we camped. Bobby and Wilmarth and Seavey came along that night. They all needed food too, and they had seen that fish. They had looked at the name on it and couldn't tell whose it was, but it wasn't theirs so they all passed it by.

Anyway, Bobby and I camped together that night. Seavey and Wilmarth kept going.

March 13 - Lost

That next day we took off and caught them up as they were getting up. We were lost by then. We didn't know where in the heck we were at. I had these maps, but I lost my location. I only knew the general area we were in. We were trying to get into Poorman, only we didn't know which way to go. Well, we all agreed on which way we should try and the guys on the snowgos took off.

Wilmarth and I left our dogs and started following them on snowshoes, just to try to find out where we were at. We must have walked two, three miles and then we got to saying, "This couldn't be it. This couldn't be the right direction." So we turned around, and when we got back to the dogs we had no more feed.

I had half a beaver that day, and one of my dogs that was on wheel I didn't have a neckline on. He had turned around and ate the half a beaver up.

The day before I had seen some moose tracks about four miles back. I had a rifle. Johnny Coffin was with us too by then, so there was five of us. Really, we had nothing for us to eat and nothing for the dogs to eat. So I told them, "Let's go back and hunt that moose." Well, moose season hadn't opened yet and the guys weren't too crazy about the idea. Anyway, Wilmarth said he would go with me, so we turned around and headed back the way we came the day before with the idea of going moose hunting. This was a creek we were heading for where the moose was hanging out.

We were heading back down there and it had cleared up. A plane started circling us. He landed right in front of us, right on the flat there, and he said, "You guys are lost." Well, we knew we were lost.

We were sure glad to see him come in. It was some friends of Wilmarth's. (Albert Tredricks and Bob Vanderpool of Red Devil. Ed.) They had that plane loaded. It was a Piper. They gave us their emergency rations and some fish and just about everything we needed. Then they took off and picked up a lot of dog food for the whole bunch of us from Ruby.

The pilots flew back to Ruby that evening, and they said they would be back in the morning to show us the way out of there to Poorman. Anyhow, we got the idea of the general direction we were supposed to head, and that evening we made camp right there in this creek.

We had four snowgos, you know, and the guys that were traveling with them just brought back three that evening. They said one of the machines had broke down and they had to leave it. It was hard going for the snowgos. They were always getting stuck in deep snow and stuff. When we came across a machine that was stuck, we'd help pull it out. We were all in this mess together.

I heard a lot this last winter about the 20-foot drifts we had in there. That was kind of a joke, really. I'd say there was between five and six feet of snow on the ground and maybe you'd be sinking down two feet of this. To tell you the truth, I've never seen a 20-foot drift in my life, unless it was a snowslide or something, and maybe not even then. But it makes a good story.

So we camped that night right there. That day we didn't make any headway at all. In fact, we went back four miles. And it was cold. I don't really know how cold, but about 30 - 40 below.

March 14 - Into Poorman

Going into Poorman we made about 20 miles. We must have got there roughly five or six in the evening. Poorman is a mining camp.

Actually we had a hard time that day, the snowgos and the whole bunch of us. The snow was soft and deep and it was tough going. But you know, I didn't mind on this. I was still enjoying myself, and everybody out there on the trail was getting along really well. What I did mind was that I knew my dogs had just about had it. They were run down and weak. They were losing weight and they weren't feeling good.

That evening about nine o'clock three guys from Ruby came in. There was Donald Stickman, he was from Galena, and Emmet Peters and Alvin Kangus from Ruby. They had heard we were coming and that we were lost. Poorman is 60 miles out of Ruby. So Donald Stickman had taken off from Galena and driven all the way up to Ruby, and there he got two more guys to go on to Poorman with him. They broke trail for us that far.

March 15 - Poorman to Ruby

The next morning Bobby took off first and I caught him while he was having coffee. I don't remember whose place that was where we had coffee. Somebody staying at a mining camp for the winter. All this time while we were going along the people were really wonderful. Like we'd come to a beaver camp or any of the villages, and we couldn't have been treated better. The whole trip was like this, all the way from Anchorage to Nome. There wasn't enough that poeple could do for you.

That day I was down to 10 dogs. Wilmarth, Vent, and Seavey got in before me. I had three dogs in the basket when I got in. The dogs were just about finished. In fact, that last day into Ruby I was thinking of calling it quits, really, because I wasn't doing these dogs any good.

That evening when Johnny came in I could see that his dogs were just about done for too. The teams that looked good at that stage were Wilmarth's and Seavey's. Their dogs looked round.

The first place I ran into the vet was in Ruby. He looked at the dogs, and that is when I found out that they had the flu. The vet gave me some antibiotics.

I left some dogs in Ruby that didn't look like they could go on. Every place that we stopped they checked how many dogs we had and how many we dropped off. The Iditarod Committee flew the dogs back to Knik. The dogs that I dropped in Ruby I just left there, and I made arrangements to get them back myself to Fairbanks.

In that tough going from McGrath to Ruby I had to use Jarvi steady. But then I had to haul him into Ruby. His feet were shot, so I had to leave him. He is back here in the yard now.

March 16 - Ruby to Galena

The next day Wilmarth and Seavey took off and I left behind them. About 10 miles below Ruby Bobby caught me up. By this time I was down to six dogs. Just six dogs left.

When I hit the Yukon there at Ruby that was just like being home to me. I mean I was really glad to be there, especially the shape my dogs were in.

Ruby to Galena is 50-odd miles. When we got into Galena that night I was pretty well discouraged. I figured that if I kept my dogs going they would never make it. And I had two of my race dogs in there yet. I didn't want to hurt them. So I figured I had to stay in Galena until they all started feeling better.

March 17, 18 - In Galena

When I stopped in Galena I found a house where I could bring my dogs in. There was an oil stove in there. I brought the dogs in the house and kept them warm and fed them every six hours. I quit commercial food altogether and went to beaver meat and rice. I stayed there for three nights, feeding them every six hours.

I started giving them penicillin shots, and then I boosted them up with vitamin shots too. Like I had liver and iron and B 12. Actually, where I got my penicillin was from the nurse's aid there, Mrs. Carroll. She was real good with her medicine. She didn't say, "Well, these are dogs. We can't use our medicine for them." She didn't say any of that. She went right ahead and gave the dogs penicillin, one a day for the three days that I was there.

After the dogs had one day's rest inside this warm house, I could see that they were full of life again. They felt like moving around. I figured they are on their way back up.

I had a hard time holding myself there. I knew the rest of the mushers were covering ground yet, but then I knew again that I had to lay my dogs up another day. After I laid them off the second day they looked good. Their eyes looked good and their stools tightened up and they looked good all around.

The six dogs I had left were Blue, you know my old leader, the one I talked about earlier in the book. She was 13 years old and about 40 pounds. I had her in single lead the last part of the race, and before that I used Little Toughie with her sometimes and Tootsie.

Tootsie was still there too. He is male, about 5 years old and 50 pounds.

Little Toughie was still there too. He is male, about 5 years old and 50 pounds.

Another dog I had was James, about 1½ years old, 45 pounds.

And Martin, about 2½ years old, 45 pounds.

And Husky. This dog was 6 years old and 50 pounds. He was the best pulling dog I had in the whole bunch, even when I started with the 16 dogs. I got him from Joe Peterson. This dog has been on a trapline all his life. He is a pulling dog. At the end, if I didn't have him, I don't know how I would have gotten along. For hauling a load, the rest of them were really a poor bunch of dogs. They had never been taught to pull. All they ever did was race. Except for this one dog they weren't like dogs we used to have, that you throw a load of wood on and they wouldn't have no problem.

March 19 - Galena to Nulato

Well, after three nights in Galena there were 11 teams ahead of me when I took off. Some were two days ahead and some were one day, and one team left just ahead of me that same day.

When I left I thought, "Well, really I don't know how tough the dogs are. How good they are feeling." So that day I caught up the team that left ahead of me.

Nulato is roughly 50 miles from Galena, and that night I camped in Nulato.

The people in Nulato were wonderful, really helpful, particularly the school kids. They got spruce boughs for the the dogs and hauled water and dried harnesses and stuff like that. Rudy Peter and his family put me up for the night.

That evening when we were sitting around I got to talking with the guys, you know, and they asked me what I figured I was going to do, where I was going to come in. Well, when I came into Nulato the dogs looked good. Nothing wrong with them. And they were making good time. But then I really didn't know how much strength they had. So I told them, "I think I could catch the guys that are a day ahead of me. But Wilmarth and Seavey and Vent that are two days ahead, I don't know if I can catch them. But, if my dogs hold up, I'll try."

"I stopped at an old cabin there that was on the map. It was pretty well broke down." John Schulz' team seen resting in front of "Ten Mile Cabin" between Kaltag and Old Woman. Casey Celusnick had been injured earlier and had to abandor the race. John went on alone with the team and finished last; but he finished. Photo by John Schulz.

March 20 - Nulato to Old Woman

The next day when I got to Kaltag the dogs looked good yet. I still had six, and I was down to a race sled.

I wasn't carrying much gear and the race sled did fine on the river. But when I took off out of Kaltag, I got off the Yukon and started making the portage over to Unalakleet. The snowgos had made the trail wavy, really bumpy. And I found out that the runners on this race sled were too long in back. The sled was hitting too hard in the front. So about 10 miles out of Kaltag I took an ax and I chopped the runners off two feet behind the back stanchions. Then it rode better.

All this time I was pushing now. I made it as easy on my dogs as I could.

I must have got roughly 50 miles out of Kaltag and I stopped at an old cabin there that was on the map. It was pretty well broke down. There was no stove or anything. But I thought I would make camp. So I started making tea. I had covered about 90 miles already that day, and these dogs, dogs that were so sick just a few days ago, they were standing there hollering to go. You know, they were hollering and jerking. There was only six of them but that is how good they were feeling. And I got to thinking, "Well, hell, this isn't a very good camp and the dogs look good yet, so I'll keep going."

So I kept going until I came to a place that they call Old Woman. It was getting fairly dark by that time, and we must have covered better than 100 miles that day.

There were two teams and a checkpoint at Old Woman. Seavey, Vent, and Wilmarth were still two days ahead of me, and Johnny Komack and Johnny Coffin and Issac Okleasik and Herbert Nayukpuk and Dick Mackey were one day ahead of me.

March 21 - Old Woman to Shaktoolik

Next morning I must have got up roughly two o'clock, and I took off about three. I traveled pretty fast that morning, and when I was coming into Unalakleet, Dick Mackey was just pulling out.

Really windy that day. We were on the coast then.

Before I got over there I had been thinking of the snow conditions. I had been traveling with this white plastic, and it was easy running all the time when the conditions were right for it. But then I figured that over there on the coast it was going to be different with salt in the snow. So I had called up Karen from Galena and told her to send every kind of ski wax she can get her hands on over to Unalakleet so it will be there when I get there.

I picked up the ski wax and stayed three hours in Ukalakleet. Before this we had a lot of ups and downs all the way from Anchorage, but when I left Unalakleet I didn't know what hills were until that day. It is 40 miles to Shaktoolik, and it seemed like we were going up all the time and it didn't take very long to come down. Anyway, I had to walk all the way up those hills.

That night about three or four miles from Shaktoolik I caught Johnny Coffin. And when I came into Shaktoolik I found Johnny Komack and Issac Okleasik and Dick Mackey and Herbert Nayukpuk. And two of the civilian snow travelers that were broke down.

The wind was really blowing.

You know my dogs were skinny. They were in pretty good shape, but I didn't think they could take that wind that night. The people in Shaktoolik were putting us up in the National Guard armory, and all of us were staying there.

There was a room in back. So what I did that night was, I just brought my six dogs in that room and tied them up in there. It was pretty warm.

March 22 - Shaktoolik to Koyuk

The next morning when we got up we couldn't leave. It was too windy. Really cold. I asked Herbert and Issac if we could go and they said, "No." You know we were in their part of the country by then, and they said, "We don't travel when it's this cold, when the wind is blowing like this. The dogs would freeze." Well, they know what they are talking about and this was all new to me, so we were storm-bound.

I think we stayed in Shaktoolik about 18 hours. Then about two in the afternoon, that's when the wind died down, we all took off again.

We covered roughly 50, 60 miles from Shaktoolik to Koyuk, and we were bucking wind all day. I took it as easy on my dogs as I could. I stayed off the sled most of that day, and I was running and pushing with my dogs all the time, just steadily.

When we had hit the bay over there at Unalakleet, the sled had started pulling hard, you know, this plastic was pulling hard. I tried all that different type of wax that I had. I tried everything on the runners, but nothing seemed to work. Today yet I don't know what would be easier. Maybe you could use iron. Maybe that might be better. Anyway, the sled was pulling hard, and even on level ground I had to pedal with one foot.

And I figured that traveling over there, there must be some salt in that snow, so I never let the dogs bite snow. I was stopping roughly every 1½, 2 hours, and every time I stopped I gave them a piece of raw meat to chew on.

We were all traveling in a bunch and I could see that my dogs weren't strong enough. Issac had the strongest dogs of all. His dogs looked good. Johnny Komack's and Dick Mackey's dogs looked pretty good too. Herbert's looked good, but Herbert only had six dogs by then too. Johnny Coffin's dogs were pretty well run down.

I could tell that I couldn't travel with these guys. They had too much power for me. I was thinking by then,

"Well, I can't leave them while I'm traveling with them. The only way I am going to leave them is while they're sleeping."

Of the six of us traveling together, I was the fifth one into Koyuk. I fed my dogs, but then I just left everything as it was. I left the dogs in their harness. This is the first time since I left Anchorage that the dogs are going to sleep in their harness. I tied my gear back into my sled, and I went into the armory to eat. I was pretty doggone pooped.

March 23 - Koyuk to White Mountain

I stayed in Koyuk three hours. I didn't take nothing out of my sled. I just laid on the floor with my clothes on and didn't have no sleeping bag or nothing. I went to sleep and woke up a couple of hours later. I was really restless by then. I wanted to get moving. My dogs were hitched up and everything was tied down. So when I woke up, I just walked out and took off. It was about midnight.

Once I got that break, once I left ahead of the others, my idea was just not to let them catch me up because I knew that if they did catch me I couldn't leave them.

It was pretty tough going really. The one snow traveler that was left had kept going to Nome. It was way ahead so there was a lot of snow on the trail.

I got into the village of Elim and was just barely staying awake. The people there were really good to me. They fed me lunch and they wanted me to sleep because I was going to sleep sitting down. But I had to keep going. I stayed about an hour, and by that time there was a radio report that the guys were two hours behind me.

So I took off again for Golovin. It was a pretty tough stretch in there. It wasn't very far, maybe 20 miles, but there was a lot of steep climbs, some of them 3, 4 miles long. Nothing but uphill.

I got into Golovin about 6, 7 o'clock in the evening, and I ate again. I stayed roughly two hours and by that time I got a radio report that the guys had pulled out of Elim. They were still two hours behind me. So I left Golovin about nine o'clock that evening.

By this time it was dark and I was heading for White Mountain. Really, you know, I didn't know where in the heck I was. I sort of had to trust the dogs to find the trail. Anyway, I got to White Mountain about midnight that night.

I figured I'd stay in White Mountain and sleep and rest until the first team came in. I knew they were two hours behind me. The three guys in front of me, Vent and Seavey and Wilmarth, I knew I couldn't catch because I got a report that they had already finished the race. But I was going to try to stay ahead of the rest of these guys.

So I asked one of the guys there at White Mountain to wake me up when the first team came in. The reason I was going to stay there was I figured that whoever comes in behind me is going to have to stop and rest for a little while too. So when he gets in, I'll just take off.

By this time it was 24 hours since I left Koyuk. I hadn't slept for 24 hours. And the last time I slept it was only for two hours.

March 24 - White Mountain to Nome

The first team that came in there to White Mountain was Herbert. He was two hours behind me, and it was roughly two o'clock in the morning. He was the only one that came in that evening. The rest of the guys stopped in Golovin. So when Herbert pulled in, I pulled out.

I tell you I had a rough time from there. I was just about sleeping on my feet.

Towards the end there I was really surprised with how little sleep the dogs could get by with, how quickly they could recover with so little rest. They were tough by then, and as long as I could stay on my feet, they could stay on their feet. Really, I don't know for sure how many hours I stopped those last three days, but as long as I was ready to go, these dogs were ready to go too. I've run dogs a long time, but their endurance really amazed me.

I think that last day was the toughest day I had from start to finish. I don't know how many miles it is from White Mountain to Nome, but about half of that is hills. And I do mean hills. Some places there was 3, 4 miles really steep. And I had to walk up all those climbs. And the sled still pulling hard. By then I was talking to myself and asking myself what I was doing out there.

Anyway, that day I got into Nome. About five o'clock in the afternoon. Herbert must have slept a little longer than I did in White Mountain because he finished five or six hours behind me.

"Anyway, that day I got into Nome. About five o'clock in the afternoon." The wheel dogs are Martin, on the left with the boot, and James. Photo by Mike McDermott.

"Lawrie and Virginia Gay had flown up and were there when I finished."
Lawrie Gay (first to the left of George's head) and Virginia (third to the left of George's head) and a host of well-wishers congratulate him on his spectacular fourth place finish.
Photo by Mike McDermott. An Anchorage Daily News photo.

UNWINDING

My dogs were feeling pretty good, you know, when we finished the race. I had left Galena two days behind Wilmarth, and I was one day behind him into Nome. Even from the last checkpoint at Solomon, which was 30 miles from Nome, I made it in roughly an hour faster than he did. You know he was the winner of the race. (Bobby Vent was second and Dan Seavey third. Ed.) So my dogs were actually in pretty good shape yet. Even at the end there, their training, that fast trotting, was paying off. They were still trotting faster than most teams when they were moving.

Blue was in better shape than any of the dogs when we got into Nome. You know I retired her in 1969 from the race team, and she had just been training pups since then. So when we started she was fat. Twenty one days later she was in good shape.

Like I said in the book earlier, for honesty you couldn't find a better dog, and that's the truth. On this trip, anything you wanted, she was there. You tell her to make a turn or something, and when you told her she would do it for you. When I got into Nome I said I had a lead dog for sale, but my price was $50,000.

Anyhow, Blue is right back here in the yard now.

When I got to Nome, I tell you I was pooped. After all this traveling I couldn't relax, couldn't unwind. It must have took me 4, 5 days to get a good night's sleep. Like I'd go to sleep and wake up. I'd keep thinking some guy was catching me up. I was uptight yet.

Actually I got there two days before I thought I would. I had told Karen I thought I would get in on Monday, but I made it on Saturday. Lawrie and Virginia Gay had flown up and were there when I finished. But when I called Karen and she tried to catch a flight, there were so many people going up to Nome about then that the flights were all booked up.

Right after the race a bunch of us were sitting around in a restaurant there in Nome just talking. The restaurant had a big picture window in front and my back was turned to the window. All of a sudden I notice that everybody is looking out this window. Well, I thought there must be a pretty girl walking by and that is the reason all these guys have stopped talking and are looking. I turned around to look too, and it was an old dog walking down the street. So that night at the banquet I brought that up and said that it seems as if we all have dogs on our minds.

But along with the kidding around and everything, there was a lot of guys that kicked after the race was over. They said like this thing was done this way and that thing shouldn't have been done that way. They were complaining, you know. I couldn't see any sense in that. I mean anybody who is going to get in a race like this knows it isn't going to be any picnic. Sure it's tough; nobody is going to baby you to Nome. But this game is supposed to be a sport. If you get beat, so what? That was the best you could do under the circumstances.

It took me months to get my dogs and everything back. After I got back to Fairbanks with part of the team - we flew the dogs back - Karen and I had to drive down to Knik and pick up the dogs we had there. Then it took quite a while to get the dogs in Ruby. We had to fly them back on commercial airlines. Every time you ship a dog up here you have to have a crate, so we had to ship crates out and all that monkeying around. And I left a lot of harnesses and stuff with Sidney Huntington in Galena. I just got those back not too long ago.

You know, I was thinking before this race started that I know just about everything there is to know about dogs. That was before the race. Well, I learned a lot.

The biggest thing I learned was the feeding. Like starting the first third of the race from Anchorage to McGrath, the dogs weren't getting enough food to hold their weight while they were traveling. And another thing was that they should have had a lot of fat on them to start with. Then, even if I didn't know how to feed them to start with, I would have had some weight to play with.

I think my race went right there on the feed. I think that if I had known how to feed the dogs they wouldn't have come down with the flu. That was a hard lesson, an $8,000 lesson, the difference between first and fourth place. Next time I won't make the same mistake.

Another thing on this race is you have got to keep your dogs happy all the time. They have got to want to do it. You can't force a dog.

Like I had one dog in there that was lazy when I started training last fall. Well, I thought, "I'll train him and make him do it." So I got the dog to work and he was a good worker, but then I had to talk to him sometimes. Every now and then I had to whip him to remind him that he's got to be working all the time.

Well, about the first three days out of Anchorage he did fine. I had him in the wheel. Then about the fourth day he found out, "Well, this son of a gun isn't going to lay a hand on me even if I don't do nothing." So he started dragging on his neckline, making the other dogs work harder. So I took his neckline off. He found out that if he slacked up enough the sled would hit him, so we went back to work. Then after I left McGrath he caught on that if he stayed right in front of the brush bow, that even if the sled did hit him, it wouldn't hit him very hard. So that's what the son of a gun did after that. He stayed right in front of the brush bow, and you can't lay a hand on him. Make the other dogs work too hard.

So there is another lesson. You can't have a lazy dog in there.

And you know, he was the one that stole that last half of the beaver that I told you about earlier. When he ate that half a beaver and I didn't have nothing left, I could have shot him right there. When I got to Ruby he was still really feeling good yet. He hadn't been doing nothing and he ate quite a bit that one day. Anyway, I was mad at him, so I gave the dog to Johnny Honea.

Looking back, I really did enjoy the trip. I didn't like laying over in McGrath and Galena, but when I was traveling I was enjoying myself. I like to be out by myself with my dogs. You know, driving dogs is my life.

The scenery was really something out there. I think the scenery alone was worth the trip.

And the people were really wonderful. All the way from Anchorage to Nome nobody would let you go through their village without having a meal. I ran into people out on their traplines who were trapping at that time of year. When you stop at their cabin there wasn't enough they could do for you. Anything you needed, anything you wanted, you could have gotten. The people were really something.

One thing this race has done is that there is more interest in dogs now in the villages. People are thinking dogs again instead of just snow machines. There are a lot of new teams starting up all over.

And from what I hear, the general public, people that were never interested in racing before, got interested just listening to this race. You know it isn't easy. It's a struggle just to get from point to point. I guess that's where the interest is. Where there's more interest, there's more dogs. So I believe that this race would do a lot of good for dog racing.

If they had another race to Nome next year, I would go again, definitely. Particularly if they had the prize money they had last year. I haven't heard of anybody who wouldn't go again.

Like Bobby Vent. That guy really suffered. He had a really bad case of arthritis and his knees were just like balloons when he got to Nome. When he was in Nome just barely getting around after the race, he said he wouldn't do it again. But after he got home in a couple of weeks he was buying all kinds of dogs. Ready to go again.

I've talked with a lot of guys that didn't compete last year. They're all going next time.

- - - - - - -

Anyway, that is just about the race I guess. I hope these tapes were what you wanted. I hope they're good enough to use for what you want them for.

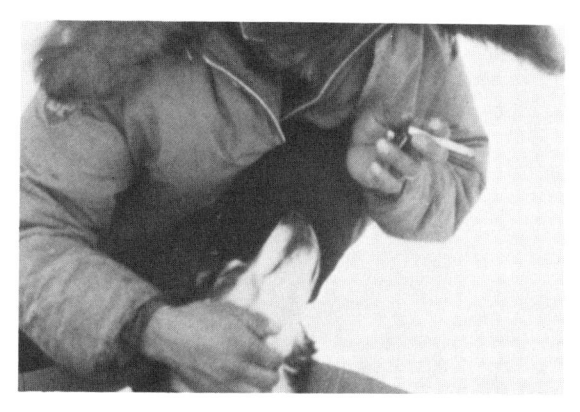

George with his 13 year old leader Blue after the finish of the race in Nome. Note the cardboard he found for her so that she wouldn't have to lie in the snow. "... for honesty you couldn't find a better dog, and that's the truth. On this trip, anything you wanted, she was there." Photograph courtesy of Art Hall, enlarged from one frame of color movie film.

COMPLETE FINAL STANDINGS
1973 IDITAROD TRAIL RACE

	MUSHER	TOTAL TIME IN Days, Hours, Minutes, Seconds
1.	Dick Wilmarth, Red Devil	20-00:49:41
2.	Bobby Vent, Huslia	20-14:08:46
3.	Dan Seavey, Seward	20-14:35:16
4.	George Attla, Fairbanks	21-08:47:53
5.	Herbert Nayukpuk, Shishmaref	21-11:00:19
6.	Issac Okleasik, Teller	21-18:21:25
7.	Dick Mackey, Wasilla	22-04:03:49
8.	John Komok, Teller	22-04:36:34
9.	John Coffin, Noorvik	23-06:43:29
10.	Ron Aldrich, Montana Creek	24-09:58:36
11.	Bill Arpino, Tok	24-12:12:00
12.	Bud Smyth, Houston	26-11:25:35
13.	Ken Chase, Anvik	26-11:45:35
14.	Ron Oviak, Point Hope	26-15:54:01
15.	Victor Katongan, Unalakleet	28-23:41:04
16.	Robert Owen Ivan, Akiak	29-11:34:25
17.	Rod Perry, Anchorage	30-01:39:21
18.	Tom Mercer, Talkeetna	31-03:35:45
19.	Terry Miller, Palmer	31-04:20:07
20.	Howard Farley, Nome	31-11:59:10
21.	Bruce Mitchell, Ester Dome	31-12:05:06
22.	John Schulz, Delta Junction	32-05:09:01